The BizBuySell Guide to Selling Your Small Business

A roadmap to the successful sale of your business

Authored by

Barbara Findlay Schenck

In Collaboration with

BizBuySell

BizBuySell Inc.
101 California Street, 43rd Fl.
San Francisco, CA 94111
www.BizBuySell.com

THIRD EDITION

Copyright © 2015 BizBuySell.
All rights reserved.

ISBN: 1475109164
ISBN 13: 9781475109160

Library of Congress Control Number: 2012906875
CreateSpace Independent Publishing Platform
North Charleston, South Carolina

The BizBuySell Guide to Selling Small Business is a roadmap to follow as you prepare to market and negotiate the sale of your small business.

Produced by BizBuySell, the Internet's Largest Business for Sale Marketplace. Written in conjunction with Small Business Strategist Barbara Findlay Schenck, author of best-selling business books *including Selling Your Business for Dummies.*

Table of Contents

THE PATH TO SELLING YOUR BUSINESS STARTS HERE

If you're thinking about selling your business, this guide is for you.

Produced by BizBuySell, the Internet's most active marketplace for businesses and franchises for sale, this guide provides a detailed overview of the small business sale process. It includes actionable advice and step-by-step instructions to follow as you prepare to exit your business by selling it to a new owner.

With over 45,000 business for sale listings and more than 1.6 million site visitors each month, BizBuySell has a unique vantage point for tracking what business buyers are seeking in today's competitive business-for-sale marketplace.

We also know that the decision to sell is often stalled by important questions, all of which this guide will help you answer:

1. Is your business ready to sell?
2. Does your business offer a compelling proposition to a new owner?
3. How much should you ask?

4. How do you launch and navigate the selling process?
5. What's involved in marketing, negotiating, financing and closing the sale?

Guide Objectives

Count on this guide to deliver:

- An overview of the business sale process
- Steps to follow as you prepare your business for sale
- Information on how to market your business for sale
- Advice regarding buyer-seller negotiations
- Information, forms and checklists to assist in financing and closing your sale
- Advice on assembling a sale team and maintaining confidentiality
- Tools for planning, offering, selling, financing and transferring your business

How To Use This Guide

This guide is comprised of five chapters, each featuring up to six sections that provide an overview of the key steps involved in selling your business and each accompanied by additional resources you can turn to for in-depth information.

Regardless of how you proceed, check back with BizBuySell regularly to receive the latest news and reports on business sales and also to receive information on guide updates. Be sure to bookmark the following website address:

http://www.bizbuysell.com/seller/guide

Guide Chapters

- Deciding why, when and how to sell your business
- Preparing your business for sale

THE PATH TO SELLING YOUR BUSINESS STARTS HERE

- Marketing your business for sale
- The selling process
- Closing the sale and transitioning your business

DECIDING WHY, WHEN AND HOW TO SELL YOUR BUSINESS

Your business has provided for your livelihood. It's created jobs, sales, revenue and marketplace visibility. And now you're ready to move on. Maybe you're seeking an exit right away. Maybe you're planning for the future. Either way, if you have questions about how to proceed, you're not alone.

Most business owners share your hesitation about how to prepare for, offer, and negotiate the sale of a small business. Most hold off because they feel they need more information and time to prepare for a sale. That's why we've produced this guide. It's also why the first chapter focuses on the issues business owners face when weighing the business-sale decision.

1

In this first chapter, five sections cover:

1. Can your business be sold?
2. What's driving your decision and why do your motivations matter?
3. How should you prioritize your wants, needs and motivations?
4. What are the various paths to a successful business sale?
5. How should you set your business sale goal and objectives?

Each section takes only minutes to review. In fact, you can read this entire guide in about an hour, though how long it will take to prepare your business for sale, and to market it, find a buyer, and negotiate a deal, will depend on your individual circumstances. This chapter helps you assess your starting point.

Key terms in this chapter:

Balance sheet: The statement of the net worth of the physical or tangible assets of your business and an indication of the value you're likely to receive should you liquidate rather than sell your business

Going concern value: The combined value of all physical assets of a business, as reflected on the balance sheet, plus the worth of the business as an ongoing entity, based on its recent past performance attracting and retaining customers and experiencing financial success.

Goodwill: The difference between the liquidation value and the going concern value of a business, reflecting the amount a buyer is willing to pay for the intangible assets of your business, including your business name and reputation, clientele, operations and systems, and marketplace advantage.

Liquidation: Ending a business by selling its physical or tangible assets to pay off creditors, with remaining proceeds distributed to the business owner or owners, and with no compensation received for the value of non-tangible assets such as business goodwill.

Seller Financing: A sale payment approach that allows the buyer to pay the business owner a portion of the selling price when the sale closes, and to pay the remainder of the price, plus interest, over a period of time specified by a loan agreement between the business owner and buyer, usually backed by security and other agreements.

CHAPTER I/SECTION I

CAN YOUR BUSINESS BE SOLD?

This section addresses the first issue you and anyone else considering a business exit faces: Is your business a good sale prospect?

In other words, will someone pay money to acquire your business or are you better off selling its physical assets and walking away?

Too many owners assume they won't find a buyer. Therefore, they automatically default to ending their businesses through liquidation. But while liquidating allows you to recapture the value of the physical or tangible assets of your business – often at fire-sale rates – it gives you nothing for the value of your business as a *going concern*.

When you sell rather than liquidate your business, a buyer pays to acquire not only the physical assets of your business – the assets listed on your balance sheet, but also to acquire the *goodwill* of your business, including the worth of such intangible assets as your business name, reputation, clientele, systems, and marketplace advantage.

The only way to harvest the value of business goodwill is through a business sale. So the decision to sell rather than to liquidate rests on a determination of whether the goodwill of your business – the value of your business beyond its physical assets – is of high enough value to attract the interest and prompt the purchase decision of a buyer.

The following steps will help you make your assessment:

Step-by-step actions

Step I. Assess the condition of your business as a sale prospect.

The following questions help you assess factors buyers consider when evaluating the worth of your business as a going concern and a purchase prospect.

Check each factor below. By answering the questions that appear you can assess whether your business is likely to be attractive to buyers or whether it needs improvement prior to a sale offering.

Sales and profit history

Yes   No

☐   ☐   Over the past 3 years, have sales revenues consistently increased?

☐   ☐   Have profits consistently increased?

☐   ☐   Have costs and operating expenses increased only at a rate consistent with revenue increases?

Yes answers indicate a recent sales and profit history that positively affects attractiveness and sale readiness of your business.

No answers indicate the need for improvement prior to a sale offering.

Financial condition

Yes   No

☐   ☐   Do the assets of your business exceed the liabilities of your business?

☐   ☐   Is your business able to consistently cover its costs and expenses from sales revenue?

Yes answers indicate that your business is financially solvent, which positively affects its attractiveness and sale readiness.

No answers indicate solvency challenges and a need to decrease debt and increase revenues and assets prior to a sale offering.

Products/Services

Yes   No

☐ ☐ Does your business offer products and/or services that are distinct and superior to those of your competitors?

☐ ☐ Does your business use a proprietary production or business process that serve as a barrier to competitors?

☐ ☐ Is your production or service delivery process one that a new owner can easily adopt and carry on?

☐ ☐ Are your production and operations processes detailed in an operations manual or other documentation?

☐ ☐ Does your business have staff and management to help a new owner successfully manage the transition after the sale of your business?

Yes answers indicate that the products and services provided and the processes employed by your business positively affect its attractiveness and sale readiness.

No answers indicate a need to improve product distinction and/or production processes and systems prior to a sale offering.

Location

Yes   No

☐ ☐ If your business relies on local or regional clientele, is it located in a market area where the number of prospective customers is increasing?

☐ ☐ Is your business located in a region with a strong and growing employee population?

☐ ☐ If your business success is reliant on its location, is it covered by a long-term and transferable lease?

☐ ☐ Do you foresee little or no threat of geographic or demographic changes that could threaten the long-term viability of your business location (for example, a train line coming through town, a nearby school closure, zoning changes, etc.)?

Yes answers indicate that your business location positively affects its attractiveness and sale readiness.

No answers indicate a need to improve your location – through a physical move or a shift in reliance on your physical location prior to a sale offering.

Facilities/Equipment

Yes   No

☐   ☐   Does your business have modern facilities and equipment?

☐   ☐   If you lease your business equipment, are leases long-term and transferable?

Yes answers indicate that your business facilities and equipment positively affect its attractiveness and sale readiness.

No answers indicate a need to consider upgrades and a lease renegotiation prior to a sale offering.

Staffing

Yes   No

☐   ☐   Other than yourself, does your business have a staff that customers or clients know and trust, which can provide continuity after your departure from your business?

☐   ☐   Have key staff members signed employee contracts that will ensure a smooth transition to a new owner?

☐   ☐   Are staffing policies outlined in an employment policy manual?

Yes answers indicate that your staffing situation positively affects its attractiveness and sale readiness.

No answers indicate a need strengthen staffing and staffing policies prior to a sale offering.

Clientele

Yes	No	
☐	☐	Does your business have a long-standing and loyal clientele?
☐	☐	Does it have a large client roster rather than reliance on a few large clients or customers?
☐	☐	Have major clients signed long-term contracts with your business?
☐	☐	Does your business maintain a customer database that a new owner can rely upon?
☐	☐	Do your customers rely on the offerings of your business more than on your own personal expertise and relationship?

Yes answers indicate that the clientele of your business positively affects its attractiveness and sale readiness.

No answers indicate a need to strengthen your clientele prior to a sale offering – by broadening your client base, maintaining a customer database, enhancing customer loyalty, and/or strengthening client relationships with your business rather than with you personally.

Brand/Reputation

Yes	No	
☐	☐	Does your business have a name that is well known and respected in its market area and business arena?
☐	☐	Does your business own its name via trademark, as a domain name and on major social media channels?
☐	☐	Does your business have strong online presence including a strong standing in search results and favourable online reviews and ratings?
☐	☐	Does your business have strong and effective marketing tools?

Yes answers indicate that your business brand and reputation positively affect its attractiveness and sale readiness.

No answers indicate a need to improve your name awareness, reputation, online presence and marketing materials prior to a sale offering.

After completing the assessments in the preceding chart, move on to Step 2.

Step 2. Flag areas of your business in need of improvement prior to a sale offering

Based on your Step 1 assessment, use the following list to flag aspects of your business that need to be strengthened prior to a sale offering.

✓ **All areas in need of improvement**

☐ Sales and profits

☐ Financial condition

☐ Products/Services

☐ Location

☐ Facilities/Equipment

☐ Staffing

☐ Clientele

☐ Brand/Reputation

Step 3. Create your pre-offering action plan and timeline

To proceed with pre-sale improvements take these steps:

1. For each area of weakness checked in Step 2, create an action plan by listing the improvements necessary to strengthen that aspect of your business. To guide your planning, refer back to Step 1. Look at

each question to which you answered *No* and create a list of actions that will allow you to switch your answer to *Yes*.

2. After creating your action plan, create a timeline for how long it will take to implement the changes you've listed.

Step 4. Decide whether to sell now, sell later, or liquidate

After assessing the attractiveness of your business as a sale prospect (Step 1), flagging areas in need of improvement (Step 2), and creating an improvement plan and timeline (Step 3), you're ready to decide between the following options:

1. Proceed with sale plans based on your positive assessment of the sale-readiness of your business

2. Invest the time and effort necessary to make your business more attractive to buyers, which will delay your sale offering, but which should lead to stronger buyer interest and a higher sale price.

3. Offer your business for sale in its current sub-optimal condition, with awareness that you'll likely receive lower buyer interest and a lower sale price. (Chapter 2/Section 5 provides pricing advice including how business conditions affect what sellers are willing to pay.)

4. Liquidate your assets based on your determination that the condition of your business will not appeal to buyers or command a price worth a sale effort.

CHAPTER I/SECTION 2

WHAT'S DRIVING YOUR DECISION?

This section helps you focus on what's motivating your sale decision and how your motivation affects the timing and approach for exiting your business.

Step-by-step actions

Step I. Define your motivation and sale urgency

Some motivations force quick action. Others allow for a more flexible timeline.

The following chart lists the motivations behind most exit plans. Use the left column to check the factors that are influencing your desire to sell your business. Then use the right column to check the urgency of your situation.

Exit Plan Motivation (✓ all that apply)	Timing (✓ to indicate your urgency
☐ You're bored by your business	☐ Immediate ☐ Flexible
☐ You feel burned out	☐ Immediate ☐ Flexible
☐ You want or need to move to a different geographic area and your business is reliant on its current location	☐ Immediate ☐ Flexible
☐ You're facing health challenges	☐ Immediate ☐ Flexible
☐ A pending or recent divorce or family or personal change prompts your need to sell	☐ Immediate ☐ Flexible
☐ You need to make more money than your business can provide	☐ Immediate ☐ Flexible

☐ Your business would benefit from increased investment and energy you don't feel able to provide	☐ Immediate	☐ Flexible
☐ You're fed up with your partners	☐ Immediate	☐ Flexible
☐ All your net worth is tied up in your business and you want to sell in order to diversify	☐ Immediate	☐ Flexible
☐ You're overwhelmed by financial problems	☐ Immediate	☐ Flexible
☐ You want to retire	☐ Immediate	☐ Flexible
☐ Other	☐ Immediate	☐ Flexible
☐ Motivations/Factors specific to you	☐ Immediate	☐ Flexible

As you consider these questions, realize that your perceived need for an immediate exit often correlates with a lower sale price for several reasons:

- If your business sale timing is immediate, you eliminate the opportunity to strengthen the attractiveness of your offering prior to a sale listing.

- If pressing financial needs force an immediate sale and payoff, you preclude your ability to offer *seller financing* which typically supports a higher selling price.

- If you want or need to make a very prompt departure from your business, you shorten or eliminate the possibility of a transition period, which likely forces a lower offer from buyers.

Step 2. Define what you want to do after a sale

Many business owners want to leave their businesses once and for all. Others want to stay involved, either as a part owner, a contract employee, or a consultant to the new owner. Often, even those who want to walk away agree to remain involved for a short period of time, usually 3-12 months, to facilitate the transition to the new owner.

Defining your after-sale interests helps you design a sale approach that fits your motivations. Consider these questions:

Yes	No	Maybe	Your personal after-sale priorities
			Do you want to sell your business and walk away?
			Are you willing to remain involved during a 3-12 month post-sale transition period?
			Do you want to remain at the managerial helm of your business after its sale?
			Do you want to remain involved full-time with your business, either as a partner or an employee, after its sale?
			Do you want to remain as a part-time consultant or employee with your business after its sale?
			Is it important (or necessary) to you to receive a full or significant payment at the time of sale closing?

Yes or *No* answers will help you determine how to offer your business for sale. *Maybe* answers indicate areas you need to consider more carefully in order to develop a sale offering that matches your desired outcome, which is the topic of Chapter 1/Section 4.

Step 3. Decide what you want for your business after a sale

Yes	No	Maybe	Your business after-sale priorities
			After a sale, is it important to you that your business remains in its current location in order to minimize disruption to your clients and to your staff?
			Is there a key employee or family member or members to whom you prefer to sell your business?
			Is there a key competitor, supplier, or other business you'd prefer (or prefer not) to sell your business?

Yes answers limit the buyer pool for your business, while *No* answers leave you open to the greatest range of prospective buyers. *Maybe* answers require additional consideration to enable you to proceed confidently with your marketing effort, which is the focus of Chapter 3.

CHAPTER I/SECTION 3

PRIORITIZING YOUR MOTIVATIONS

The preceding section in this chapter focused on the issues behind your desire
to sell your business. This section helps you prioritize your motivations.

Step-by-step actions

Step I.   State your sale motivations

The following chart lists the desired outcomes of most business owners
entering the sale process. Using a 1-10 rating, indicate how important each
objective is to you.

Low priority ←→ High priority	Your Sale Objectives
1 2 3 4 5 6 7 8 9 10	Immediate sale
1 2 3 4 5 6 7 8 9 10	Immediate departure (vs. 3-12 month post-sale involvement in business transition)
1 2 3 4 5 6 7 8 9 10	High sale price
1 2 3 4 5 6 7 8 9 10	All-cash payoff at closing (no seller-financing)
1 2 3 4 5 6 7 8 9 10	Post-sale involvement with your business
1 2 3 4 5 6 7 8 9 10	Post-sale priorities, such as little or no disruption to clients or staff
1 2 3 4 5 6 7 8 9 10	Pre-sale preparation followed by future sale

Step 2.   Resolve conflicts between your motivations.

Once you have a good sense of what you want to achieve from a sale, you'll
need to prioritize your motivations. For instance, if you want a quick sale

and a high selling price but your business isn't in top shape for a sale, you'll have to concede on either timing or price.

The following chart describes how various sale objectives conflict with one another.

Motivation	Conflicting Motivations	Why?
Immediate sale	High price	Unless business is in strong condition, an immediate sale likely requires a discounted price.
	All-cash payoff	Cash payoffs usually require buyers to seek third-party loans, which are rare and slow the sale process.
Immediate departure (vs. 3-12 month post-sale involvement in business transition)	High price	Unless business is in strong condition and easy to transition, rapid departure raises buyer doubts and leads to lower selling prices.
	All-cash payoff	Sellers seeking rapid departure and all-cash payoff create buyer doubt by telegraphing high desire to sell and/or low confidence in the future of the business.
High price	All-cash payoff	Sales involving seller financing typically close at considerably higher prices than those requiring payoff at closing.
	Immediate departure	Sellers' desire for immediate departure signals high sale desire, prompting price negotiation.
	Post-sale involvement and priorities	Post-sale requirements narrow buyer pool and decrease ability to receive highest price.

All-cash payoff at closing (No seller financing)	Immediate sale	Cash payoffs usually require buyers to seek third-party loans, which are difficult to obtain and slow the sale process.
	High price	Sales involving seller financing typically close at considerably higher prices than those requiring payoff at closing.
	Immediate departure	Sellers seeking rapid departure and full payoff at closing telegraph high desire to sell and/or low confidence in the future of the business, lowering business attractiveness to buyers.
Post-sale involvement with your business	High price	Seller's request for ongoing involvement narrows buyer pool and triggers price negotiation.
Post-sale priorities, such as little or no disruption to clients or staff	High price	Desire to keep business in current location and configuration reduces the option of merger or consolidation, narrows the buyer pool, and affects pricing.
Pre-sale preparation followed by future sale	No conflicts	With a mid- to long-term timeframe, seller can improve business condition and plan an offering that addresses objectives without conflicting priorities.

Step 3. Finalize your motivation priorities

Reviewing the motivations you indicated in Step 1 and the potential conflicts indicated in Step 2, prioritize your expectations. This will prepare you to select the best route for your business exit and sale offering, which is the topic of the next chapter in this guide.

So, what do you want? Realizing that you can't have it all, which *one* of the following objectives is your highest priority in a sale?

Your Top Sale Priority

✓ *Only one*

☐ *An immediate departure*

☐ *The highest price possible*

☐ *All-cash payoff at closing*

☐ *Post-sale involvement with your business*

☐ *Post sale priorities such as little or no disruption to clients or staff*

☐ *Pre-sale preparation followed by future sale*

CHAPTER I/SECTION 4

THE VARIOUS ROUTES TO SUCCESSFUL BUSINESS SALES

The preceding section of this guide helped you zero in on your top priority for a sale. This section outlines the various routes to business sales, with each route accompanied by a list of the seller priorities the approach achieves.

Step-by-step actions

Step I. Find the sale approaches that best match with your sale motivations

This chart helps you align your motivations with various sale approaches.

Begin on the top right side of the chart, focusing on the entry that reflects your top priority, for instance (an immediate sale or highest-possible price). Checkmarks indicate which sale approaches are most apt to achieve your desired outcome. For help setting and prioritizing your motivations, see Chapter 1/Section 3.

SALE APPROACHES	SELLER MOTIVATIONS					
	Immediate Sale	Immediate Departure	Highest Possible Price	All-Cash Payoff	Post-Sale Involvement	Post-Sale Priorities
Sell to an existing partner	✓	✓		✓	✓	✓
Sell partially to a new co-owner or partner				✓	✓	✓
Sell all or partially to a supplier, competitor or other business			✓	✓	✓	
Sell to an outside individual	✓	✓	✓	✓	✓	✓
Transition to next-generation family		✓			✓	✓
Sell to key employee					✓	✓
Sell to employees					✓	✓
Liquidate	✓	✓		✓		

Step 2. Understand what's involved with each sale approach

Once you determine which sale approaches align best with your sale objectives, you're ready to zero in on the approach that seems to fit your business and personal situation best.

Selling to an existing partner

- *Approach:* Most partnerships are launched with legal documents that include a buy-sell agreement outlining how one partner will sell to the other or others. If your partnership includes such an agreement, it details the price and procedure for selling your portion of ownership.

- *Selling advantages:* Depending on circumstances, selling to an existing partner allows a pre-defined route for selling, departing and receiving a payoff, and likely results in little disruption to clients or staff.

Selling to another business

- *Approach:* Businesses or private equity groups acquire businesses – in full or in part – for strategic rather than purely financial reasons. They aren't looking to fund a new owner's salary, but rather to integrate the offerings of the purchased business in order to expand the capabilities, market reach, competitiveness and profitability of an established business that is usually larger and stronger than the business being purchased.

- *Selling advantages:* A business-to-business sale allows the possibility of a strong selling price and potential for an immediate payoff, though the sale terms often require your ongoing involvement with your business.

Selling to an individual

- *Approach:* Individuals buy rather than start businesses to avoid start-up risk, to enjoy the immediate benefits of sales and cash flow, and to benefit from established systems, clientele, and reputation. Also, thanks in part to seller financing, it's easier to finance a business purchase than a business start-up.

- *Selling advantages:* If your business is in strong condition and attractive to buyers, selling to an individual provides the greatest opportunity to achieve the greatest range of sale objectives, so long as you keep in mind that some objectives conflict with others. For example, the need for all-cash at closing rarely supports a high selling price.

Transitioning to next-generation family members

- *Approach:* This sale approach is followed by roughly a third of all small business owners who work with their attorneys and account-ants to determine the often-complex plans for valuation, business transfer and related estate planning issues.

- *Selling advantages:* While a sale to family members takes advance planning, requires a generous timeframe, and rarely achieves a top-dollar payoff, ultimately it allows the seller flexibility in determin-ing future involvement and usually provides continuity for staff and clients.

Selling to a key employee

- *Approach:* This sale approach transitions ownership to an employee who wants and is able to make the necessary investment to take over your business. It typically begins with a legally binding part-nership and buy-sell agreement that details the terms of the sale at some point in the future.

- *Selling advantages:* Like an inner-family sale, selling to a key employee rarely achieves a top-dollar price, but ultimately it allows the seller flexibility in determining future involvement and likely provides ongoing continuity for staff and clients.

Selling to employees

- *Approach:* A sale to employees involves a tax-qualified, defined employee benefit plan, called an Employee Stock Ownership Plan (ESOP), through which employees buy shares of the business quickly or over a long period of time, depending on how the transi-tion is structured.

- *Selling advantages:* Though an ESOP requires significant legal planning and advice, it is a tax-advantageous sale approach since proceeds may be tax-free. It also allows a phase-out of the owner's involvement and provides ongoing continuity for staff and clients.

Liquidating your business

- *Approach:* Liquidation involves selling assets (possibly with assistance from liquidation sale experts), collecting outstanding receivables, paying off debts, addressing contractual commitments, releasing employees, and finalizing legal and financial obligations to close your business.

- *Selling advantages:* For owners of small businesses with significant weaknesses or solvency issues who seek immediate business exits, liquidation is likely the easiest and fastest way to recover some value and invest no further funds or efforts before leaving the business behind.

There are two other approaches for selling a small business: Merging with another business or going public through an initial public offering or IPO. Both these approaches require significant legal and accounting assistance outside the range of advice in this guide.

CHAPTER I/SECTION 5

SETTING YOUR GOAL AND OBJECTIVES

This section consists of only one step: Setting your sale goal and objectives.

Based on your knowledge of your business condition, your exit motivations and priorities, and your preferred sale approach, the following form helps you put your sale desires into words. By completing the form below, you create a statement of precisely the outcome you seek to achieve through the sale of your business.

Sale Goal

State your desired sale outcome.

- ☐ To sell my business in part and remain involved with its operation
- ☐ To sell my business in full and remain involved with its operation
- ☐ To sell my business in full and end involvement with its operation
- ☐ Other_____

Timing Objective

Indicate the timeline you seek.

- ☐ Immediate (0-6 months)
- ☐ Within a year
- ☐ Within 1-3 years
- ☐ Other _____

Financial Outcome Objective

Define your preliminary financial expectations.

Pricing: How much you can ask for your business depends on its pre-sale condition. Most businesses sell at a multiple of 1-4 times annual earnings, also called cash flow or seller's discretionary earnings, with the multiple based on business condition and attractiveness to buyers. Chapter 2/Section 5 provides pricing information. For now, consider the following questions to arrive at a preliminary pricing multiple for your business sale:

- ☐ My business is in strong condition and likely to command a high sale multiple
- ☐ I'm prepared to accept a lower pricing multiple due to the current condition of my business
- ☐ I'm willing to commit time and effort to strengthen my business condition and therefore to improve its likely pricing multiple

Pay-out:

- ☐ I'm willing to provide a seller-financed loan for a portion of the sale price
- ☐ I require an all-cash payoff at closing

Sale Approach Objectives

Prospective Buyer: Have you already defined your likely buyer or are you interested in selling to any qualified buyer, whether a business or an individual?

- ☐ I prefer or am obligated to sell to a partner, key employee, employee group or family member. (If so, you won't need to list or market your business for sale. Instead, you'll work with legal and financial advisors as you pursue next steps.)
- ☐ I intend to pursue a sale to a targeted business such as a supplier, competitor or strategic business buyer. (If so, you won't need to list your business for sale. Instead, you'll work with legal and financial advisors as you strategically market your business to select targets.)
- ☐ I seek to sell to any buyer who has the financial and managerial capability to buy my business. (If so, proceed with the following parts of this guide as you prepare to, list, market, and sell your business.)

After-sale Objectives

Your Personal Departure Objective

☐ I want to stay involved with my business in a managerial capacity after its sale.

☐ I'm willing to remain involved over a post-sale transition period of 3-12 months.

Your Post-Sale Objective for your Business

☐ I prefer to sell to a buyer who plans to retain employees and therefore cause little disruption in their lives.

☐ I'm willing to sell to a buyer with plans to merge, move or significantly alter the business.

Once you answer these questions, which may take some soul searching and careful consideration, you'll be clear about what you want from your business sale. You may end up adjusting some of your objectives along the way, but the outcome of this step puts your sale goal into words and sets your sale effort in the right direction.

CHAPTER I/CONCLUSION

Congratulations! You've now concluded the first chapter in the BizBuySell Guide to Selling Your Small Business.

- In Section 1 you assessed the strengths and weaknesses of your business as a sale offering
- In Section 2 you considered the personal motivations driving your interest in a business sale
- In Section 3 you prioritized your motivations
- In Section 4 you aligned your motivations with likely sale approaches
- In Section 5 you compiled your sale goal and objectives

Now you're ready to prepare your business for sale, which is the topic of Chapter 2.

CHAPTER 2

PREPARING YOUR BUSINESS FOR A SALE

Overview

The minute you decide to sell your business, you face two choices:

Are you going to proceed immediately, offering it for sale in its current condition, realizing you may need to make price concessions to account for unaddressed weaknesses?

Are you going to delay your sale offering until you've invested the effort and funds necessary to overcome its weaknesses and improve its attractiveness to prospective buyers?

Your answers depend entirely on your personal motivations (see Chapter 1/Section 2), and your own goals and objectives (see Chapter 1/Section 5).

Once you've clearly defined what you want and need to achieve, the information in this chapter will help you plan and implement the steps you need to follow as you prepare your business for sale.

In five sections, Chapter 2 covers:

1. Your pre-sale to do-list
2. The necessary documentation
3. Choosing your sale team
4. Pricing your business
5. Preparing a selling memo

Count on this chapter to guide you through the sale-preparation process.

Key terms in this chapter:

Purchase Price/Valuation: What your business is likely to sell for based on a buyer's assessment of financial statements, industry comparable sale figures, asset values, return on investment, and the goodwill worth of your business as a going concern. The purchase price is usually less than the asking price and the subject of seller-buyer negotiations. In fact, of the thousands of closed small business transactions reported to BizBuySell each year, businesses usually sell for arout 90% of their asking price.

Seller Financing: A payment approach that allows the buyer to pay the seller a portion of the purchase price at the time of sale closing and to pay the remainder of the price, plus interest, over a period of time specified by a loan agreement between the buyer and seller. Seller-financed loans are usually backed by security and other agreements that often use the business itself as collateral, so if the buyer fails to make payments, the seller will get the business back.

Third-Party Financing: A financing approach involving a loan provided to a buyer by a traditional lender (i.e., a commercial bank), often under a loan guarantee program through the Small Business Administration (SBA).

Performance Clauses and Earnouts: A pricing approach that attaches a portion of the sale price to the future performance of the business. This payment structure is often employed in the sale of businesses that have recently undergone a recent surge or decline in revenue or profitability, making a purchase price based on current annual earnings a weak indicator of future business value. This pricing approach is also used when a large portion of revenue is tied to a few large clients.

Seller's Discretionary Earnings: Also called annual earnings or cash flow. A re-cast income statement that reflects revenues and all essential operating costs without extraordinary, one-time or discretionary expenditures; therefore, accurately presenting how much money the business actually generates for the benefit of its owner.

CHAPTER 2/SECTION I

YOUR PRE-SALE TO-DO LIST

Get ready to get organized for your sale.

This section provides information on all the activities you need to undertake before actually presenting your sale offering. It includes:

- Information on how to prepare your business for a sale.

- Worksheets to use as you determine pre-sale improvement tasks.

- Advice for setting your pre-sale improvement plan timeline and task assignments.

The following steps guide you through the preparation process.

Step-by-step actions

Step 1. Flag the areas of your business in need of pre-sale improvement.

Buyers prefer businesses that come with low risks and high rewards.

The following chart lists aspects of your business that buyers will look at when considering it for a possible purchase. For each aspect, check whether your business condition is strong, adequate, or in need of improvement.

- *Aspects of your business that are in good condition* will contribute to a stronger offering and likely a higher price.

- *Adequacies* will contribute to an average-to-below-average price.

- *Areas in need of improvement* will likely force you to offer price concessions (unless they are offset by considerable strengths in areas of greater importance to the ongoing success of your business).

Good	Average	Poor	
			Legal Condition
			Clear ownership of assets
			Long-term, transferable leases
			No liens/claims/encumbrances
			No pending litigation/labor issues/law violations
			Up-to-date licenses
			No zoning issues
			Financial Condition
			Increasing revenues
			Increasing profits
			Positive cash flow
			Taxes paid to date
			Current debt payments
			Current receivables
			Professionally produced financial statements
			Business Image
			Trademarked name

			Reputable image
			Quality advertising
			Website/online presence
			Business location and interior
			Signage
			Publicity offline and online
			Networks/associations
			Word of mouth
			Business Operations and Organization
			Equipment
			Established, trained staff
			Well-documented operations and systems
			Profitable business model
			Key employees with transferable employment contracts
			Products
			Distinct, competitive products
			Distinct, competitive services
			Packaging/product presentation
			Proprietary production process

			Clientele
			Long-term, frequent customers
			Long-term client contracts
			Many vs. a few customers
			Loyal clientele
			Transferability
			Easy-to-transfer clientele
			Easy-to-adopt systems
			Long-term, transferable leases

Step 2. Commit to a pre-sale improvement action plan.

Using the Step 1 chart, study each aspect of your business that you indicated needs improvement. If you also answer "yes" to the following four questions the weakness should become a target of your pre-sale improvement plan:

Yes	No	
		Is the weakness in an area of high importance to the success of your business?
		Is the weakness likely to lessen a buyer's interest or affect the price a buyer is likely to offer?
		Is the cost of improving the condition likely to be less than the price concession the weakness is likely to force?
		Can you implement necessary changes within the timeframe of your sale goal?

Step 3. Create your pre-sale improvement plan.

Create an action plan for each weakness you intend to overcome. Include:

- The necessary steps you commit to take.

- The timeline you'll follow.

- The resources you'll commit to the effort.

- How you'll assign tasks in order to complete improvements by the time you intend to launch the marketing of your business for sale.

Step 4. As you strengthen your business for presentation to buyers, keep your sale plans as quiet as possible.

Share your sale intentions with key staff and outside consultants only as necessary and only when the news is accompanied by a non-disclosure or confidentiality agreement. Even when working with your financial and legal advisors, whose professional relationships are committed to confidentiality, stress the importance of keeping your sale intentions private. Should word get out that you plan to sell your business, you risk creating uncertainty among employees, customers and suppliers, which can devalue your business at the same time you most need to increase its worth.

Resources:

Article, *Keeping it Confidential*;

http://www.bizbuysell.com/seller_resources

For in-depth assistance read:

The book, *Selling Your Business for Dummies*, devotes several chapters to the steps involved in the pre-sale improvement process.

The book, *Built to Sell*, which details how to build and sell a profitable, automated, efficient business.

CHAPTER 2/SECTION 2

THE NECESSARY DOCUMENTATION

Sooner or later your prospective buyer will expect – or, put more accurately, the buyer will demand – to see "just the facts" about your business.

This section guides you through assembly of the documentation you need to be ready to share.

Step 1. Be aware of the documents you'll need to present during the sale process.

You may already have many of these documents complete and available, in which case you can check *Ready* to the left of the document description. Otherwise, check *Need* and plan to work with professional sale team members (described in the next section of this chapter) so you'll be prepared when the documentation is needed.

DOCUMENTS REQUIRED IN THE SMALL BUSINESS SALE PROCESS					
Ready	Need	Document	Ready	Need	Document
		Non-Disclosure Confidentiality Agreement			Business Formation Documents
		Personal Financial Statement Form for Buyer to Complete			Corporate or Schedule C Tax Returns for Past 2-3 Years
		Offer-to-Purchase Agreement			Building or Office Lease

		Note for Seller Financing			Equipment Leases and Maintenance Agreements
		Financial Statements for the Current and Past 2-3 Years			Business Licenses, Certifications and Registrations
		Statement of Seller's Discretionary Earnings or Cash Flow			Professional Certificates
		Financial Ratios and Trends			Insurance Policies
		Accounts Payable and Accounts Receivables Aging Reports			Copies Proving Ownership of Patents, Trademarks and Other Intellectual Property
		Inventory List with Value Detail			Outstanding Loan Agreements
		List of Fixtures, Furnishings and Equipment with Value Detail			Description of Liens
		Asset Depreciation Schedule from Tax Return			Product/Service Descriptions and Price Lists
		Supplier and Distributor Contracts			Business Plan

		Client List and Major Client Contracts			Marketing Plan and Samples of Marketing Materials
		Staffing List with Hire Dates and Salaries; Employment Agreements			Employment Policy Manual
		Organization Chart			Business Procedures Manual
		Photos of Business			Other Documents Unique to Your Business
		List of Opportunities for Improvement with Revenue/Profit Projections for Each			Other
		Other			Other

Step 2. Assemble all documents so you're ready when the need arises – and it will!

The business description that you provide in early ads and communications will draw initial buyer interest, and your early personal assurances and explanations will inspire further interest. But it's highly unlikely that you'll receive any kind of interest commitment, let alone an offer or indication of purchase intention, until you turn over hard-copy versions explaining provable facts, figures, and financial statements for your business.

Begin immediately to assemble all the documentation you'll need over the time period in front of you.

Resources:

Article, *Keeping it Confidential*; http://www.bizbuysell.com/seller_resources

Article, *Documents and Information Required for Selling a Business*; http://www.bizbuysell.com/seller_resources

CHAPTER 2/SECTION 3

CHOOSING YOUR SALE TEAM

Selling your business is one of those things that is difficult to do alone.

You will likely find yourself needing help preparing your sale offering, marketing your business, producing financial and other documents that buyers require, and completing the legal papers that protect you, your business, and your buyer after the final handshake.

Here's a glance at the sale process and where advisors fit in:

	Decision to Sell	Prepration for a Sale	Pricing	Marketing	Due Dilligence	Negotiation	Closing!
YOU	✓	✓	✓	✓	✓	✓	✓
Accountant	✓	✓			✓	✓	
Appraisers			✓				
Attorney		✓			✓	✓	
Broker		✓	✓	✓	✓	✓	✓
Consultants		✓					

Every business sale involves a team, though the team players vary depending on the nature and complexity of your business, your abilities and experience, and the amount of energy and time you can/are willing to devote to the effort (As a seller who still has a business to operate, the one thing you can't afford is a business performance down-turn!).

Here are the steps to follow as you decide who to involve.

Step-by-step actions

Step 1. Decide who you want on your business-sale team.

Some business owners handle the process of selling their businesses with assistance only from their attorney and accountant. Others seek assistance from appraisers, brokers, and business consultants.

The following questions help guide your decisions.

DO YOU NEED...?	YOUR ANSWER IS LIKELY TO BE *YES* IF...
An appraiser or valuation expert?	Your business involves intellectual property, proprietary processes, a valuable brand or other assets that are difficult to value and price *Note: Some business brokers also provide general valuation services so, if you are using a business broker, you may not need a separate appraiser.*
Consultants?	Your selling price could be significantly higher if you implemented major business improvements beyond the expertise of you and your management team
A broker?	You don't have experience selling a business or, and even if you do, you don't have the time to both run your business and sell it without business performance suffering; you're not the best person to market, present and negotiate the sale of your business; your likely buyers are difficult to target and reach

Step 2. Determine whether and how to hire a broker.

If you decide to market your business on your own, your offering is considered "for sale by owner" or FSBO (pronounced, "fizbo"). Typically an owner goes the FSBO route in one of the following scenarios:

- Owner cannot find a broker interested in representing his/her business for sale

- Owner cannot afford or does not want to pay the success fee/ broker's commission (which usually is 10% of the final purchase price, but can be more for smaller deals or less for bigger deals)

- Owner feels they can handle the process themselves and/or wants to maintain complete control of the process

Even though you *can* go it alone, however, doesn't mean you won't benefit greatly from the involvement of a broker who can assist you with the business selling process. For starters, business brokers are advisors who offer in-depth insights on valuation, marketing, prospecting, negotiations, and other fundamental sale elements. Most brokers have extensive prior business experience that allows them to understand the financial, operational, and legal issues of your company. Their role as a sale facilitator will help streamline the process, allowing them to focus on the deal while you continue to operate the business.

Among the good reasons to hire assistance, consider that professional intermediaries provide the following benefits:

- They can be a good buffer between you and the buyer.

- They can handle the flow of documentation.

- They have done it before and have likely dealt with most challenges that can arise.

When hiring a broker, be aware that there are two main types of business sale intermediaries. Businesses worth more than several million dollars are usually sold by mergers and acquisitions (M&A) specialists while smaller businesses typically work with business brokers.

When seeking a qualified broker to help sell your business, be sure to check out BizBuySell's Broker Directory which includes thousands of qualified professionals who can help sell your business.

Business Brokers have different strengths and weaknesses depending on their reaching background and experiences. You will likely need to interview several different brokers before reaching a decision.

Use the following questionnaire to record answers from your broker interviews:

Questions to ask brokers	Space to note broker responses
Experience --Length of time in business? --Full time or part time? --Independent or part of a broker group? --IBBA or CBI Certified?	
Performance Record --Number of annual listings? --Number of annual sales? --Average sale price compared to asking price? --Experience with businesses similar to yours?	
Web Presence --Broker's site traffic? --Number of buyers in broker database?	
Marketing Plan --How your business will be priced? --How your listing will be marketed? --How broker uses online business-for-sale listing sites?	

Questions to ask brokers	Space to note broker responses
Contractual Arrangements --What is the broker's fee? (usually 10 % of purchase price or a pre-set fee, whichever is greater) --Does the broker charge a cancellation fee if you withdraw the listing; or a trailing fee if after the listing expires you sell to a buyer referred by the broker? --Does broker allow carve-outs or exclusions that reduce fees if your business sells to a person you named as a potential buyer at the time of the listing?	
References --Will the broker provide names and contact information so you can interview clients?	

Step 3. Contact business appraisers or valuation specialists if your business is difficult to price.

If you work with a business broker or intermediary, most will help you determine the value of your business and set an asking price. In some instances, however, you may need to involve a business appraiser.

If you're seeking advice on the value of the real property of your business, turn to a real estate appraiser. For help valuing your entire business, you'll want to seek advice from a business appraiser, and preferably one with a professional designation from a reputable and recognized trade association. Look for an appraiser with one of the following credentials:

43

- CBA/Certified Business Appraiser

- ASA Accredited Senior Appraiser

- CPA/ABV Certified Public Accountant Accredited in Business Valuation

- CVA Certified Valuation Analyst

- CBV Chartered Business Valuator

Search online and seek industry advice for qualified appraisers in your business field, or ask your attorney accountant or business broker, who can refer you to a trusted, experienced appraiser in your industry or market area.

Step 4. Remember, confidentiality is key during the sales process.

Customers, competitors, suppliers, employees and creditors all will have different reactions if they learn that your business is for sale. Even buyer prospects often react negatively to a business opportunity that has not been kept confidential.

Chapter 3/Section 1 details how to protect confidentiality when dealing with prospects. But, even before dealing with buyers, remember to obtain confidentiality agreements when dealing with sale advisors and other confidants. Otherwise, you risk disturbing the confidence of your staff, suppliers or customers, which is the last thing you want when you're working to keep your business strong for a potential sale.

Resources:

Article, *Choosing a Business Appraiser* http://www.bizbuysell.com/seller_resources

Article, *Should You Sell It Yourself or Hire an Intermediary?* http://www. bizbuysell.com/seller_resources

Article, *Finding the Right Business Broker for Your Business Sale*; http://www. inc.com/curtis-kroeker/

CHAPTER 2/SECTION 4

SETTING YOUR ASKING PRICE

Anyone considering a business sale faces the same question: How much is my business worth? This section helps you come up with your answer.

Step 1: Get your financial statements in order.

If by any chance you keep your business records in a check book register or shoebox, here's what you absolutely have to do before pricing your business for a sale: You have to assemble formal financial records for your business for this year and the previous three years (if your business is that old).

Unless you're skilled in accounting, work with a bookkeeper or accountant to prepare the following forms:

- **Income statement** showing your gross revenue, costs, and how much your business made or lost each year

- **Cash flow statement** showing how money was received and paid out of your business and how business assets changed as a result

- **Balance sheet** showing the value of all tangible assets owned by your business less the liabilities your business owes.

- **Seller's discretionary earnings statement**, also called the owner's cash flow, showing how much your business makes after backing out non-recurring and discretionary expenses as described in Step 3.

Step 2: Estimate the value of the tangible assets of your business.

It's essential to list and price all physical assets of your business, including furnishings, fixtures, equipment and inventory, for two reasons:

- The worth of tangible assets is important to business buyers, who will require you to provide a complete asset list, including purchase prices and current market values.

- The worth of tangible assets is also important to you, because if you determine that the value of the assets of your business is very similar to the price you're likely to receive through a sale – which you'll calculate following the next two steps – you may decide liquidation is a more expedient route to recovering value from your business investment.

Step 3: Prepare your statement of seller's discretionary earnings.

To calculate your business asking price, you first need to work with your accountant, bookkeeper or business broker to recast your business income statement into what's interchangeably called a statement of owner's cash flow or a statement of seller's discretionary earnings (SDE). Under either name, it is the basis for sale pricing and of primary interest to buyers.

Following is a sample of an SDE statement.

It differs from an income statement in two ways:

- The income statement reflects the full range of normal and legal deductions, resulting in the lowest-possible bottom line and taxable profit

- The SDE or owner's cash flow statement presents the full earning power of your business after adding back in one-time, non-recurring purchases and discretionary expenses shown on your income statement but not essential to business operations.

In the following example, shaded cells indicate areas where the income statement is adjusted to reflect earning potential – called *recasting* or *normalizing* your financials.

Annual Seller's Discretionary Earnings	$
Annual Revenue	
Annual Cost of Sales	
Annual Expenses	
Annual Net Income	
Adjustments for Interest, Depreciation, Tax and Amortization deductions	
Add-back for Interest paid on loans	
Add-back for Depreciation	
Add back for Taxes paid	
Add back for Amortization	
EBIDTA (Earnings before Interest, Depreciation, Taxes and Amortization)	
Adjustments for Personal, Discretionary and One-Time Expenses	
Add-back for Owner's Salary, Payroll Tax, Benefits	
Add-back for Family Member Wages, Payroll Tax, Benefits	
Add-back for Owner/Family Personal Auto Use	
Add-back for Contributions/Donations	
Add-back for Fair-Market Rent Adjustment	
Add-back for Owner's Insurance premiums	
Add-back for Legal, Accounting, Tax services	
Add-back for Owner Retirement Plan contributions	

Annual Seller's Discretionary Earnings	$
Add-back for Travel/Entertainment Expenses	
Add-back for Subscriptions and Memberships	
Add-back for extraordinary, one-time, non-recurring expenses reflected on Income statements	
Adjusted Statement of Projected Annual Seller's Discretionary Earnings	

Step 4: Estimate the earnings multiple that's likely to apply when pricing your business.

Most small businesses sell based on an earnings multiple of 1-4. Translated, that means most owners receive somewhere between one and four times the annual SDE of their businesses, with the multiple pegged to the attractiveness of the business being purchased.

To begin to estimate where on the 1-4 range your business attractiveness is apt to fall, use the following chart:

Attribute	Rate Your Business from 1 (lowest) to 4 (highest)
Recent Performance: Over past 2-3 years did your business revenues and profits increase steadily (highest), or were they flat (average) or declining (lowest)?	
Ease of Transition: Does your business have policies, procedures, systems and staff that will make a new owner's transition very easy (highest) or difficult (lowest)?	

Attribute	Rate Your Business from 1 (lowest) to 4 (highest)
Financial Records: Does your business have clean, complete, accurate financial statements that reflect all income (highest) or are your records informal and not inclusive of all your business revenue (lowest)?	
Clientele: Do you have a broad base of profitable clients with no client representing more than 5% of your revenues, and do you have good customer lists and contracts (highest) or do a few customers account for most sales, without customer lists or strong, transferable contracts (lowest)?	
Products: Does your business offer distinctly different, better, and difficult-to-copy products and services; does it serve an exclusive territory; does it offer an exclusive product line under transferable contracts or arrangements (highest) or does it offer products identical to those offered by other businesses in your market area with no distinct competitive advantage (lowest)?	
Recurring Revenue: Does your business sell via subscriptions, monthly fees, automatic delivery programs or other approaches that deliver ongoing revenue from established customers (highest) or are most sales single-time transactions by one-time or occasional customers (lowest)?	

Attribute	Rate Your Business from 1 (lowest) to 4 (highest)
Staffing: Does your business have key staff with transferable contracts who will assist with the business transition (highest) or are you the one-and-only key person (lowest)?	
Location: If your business success is reliant on its location, is it located in a growing and desirable market area and in a location with a long-term, transferable lease and good facilities and equipment (highest), or will a new owner need to move or improve the location (lowest)?	
Brand and Reputation: Does your business have a well-known name, respected reputation, and top-position within its competitive arena (highest) or are the reputations of competitors considered stronger and preferable (lowest)?	

After completing this chart, you'll begin to understand the probable attractiveness of your business to buyers. If it is strong in areas of high importance to its current and future success, it's likely to command a higher-than-average earnings multiple. Conversely, if it's weak in key areas, buyers will assess its worth at a lower-than-average multiple when arriving at a purchase price offer.

Step 5: Do the math to arrive at an early estimate of your purchase price.

Based on how attractive your business appears in key areas that most affect its future success under new ownership, you can multiply your annual seller's discretionary earnings (from Step 2) by your estimated earnings multiplier (from Step 4) to arrive at a preliminary estimation of your business purchase price.

Realize this early price estimate will likely be adjusted before you present it for two reasons:

- You may not be the best person to assess the attractiveness of your business to buyers, which is why outside intermediaries and assessors are so valuable.

- Your asking price needs to account for the fact that buyers negotiate downward. Of the thousands of closed small business transactions reported to BizBuySell each year, most businesses sell for about 90% of their asking price. Your asking price will need to account for that variance without stating a number so high that it reduces buyer interest and inquiries.

Your asking price must be in line with prices of comparable business sales, which is the topic of the next step.

Step 6: Do some price checking

After arriving at your estimated purchase price, conduct the following research:

- On the www.bizbuysell.com home page use the search boxes to find information on recent listings and sales in your business category, market area, and price range. The findings will help you determine what businesses like yours are going for and what separates one business from the next in terms of what the owner is asking for the business. Keep in mind that these are only asking prices, and they are no guarantee that the business will actually sell for the asking price.

- Use the BizBuySell Valuation Report Tool (http://www.bizbuysell. com/business-valuation-report/) to gain insights into the selling prices of comparable businesses and to determine a likely asking price for your business. Via this low-cost report, you can see actual transaction prices of local businesses, and include or exclude the comps you choose to get a sampling that best reflects your business.

- Work with your sale advisors, including your broker if you're using one, or with industry association contacts if available, to see how your pricing estimate syncs with the prices of recent comparable-business sales.

Resources:

Helpful Tool, BizBuySell Valuation Report http://www.bizbuysell.com/business-valuation-report

Article, *What Impacts the Purchase Price of a Business for Sale;*

http://www.bizbuysell.com/seller_resources

Article, *Valuation Rules of Thumb* http://www.bizbuysell.com/seller_resources

Article, Choosing a Business Appraiser http://www.bizbuysell.com/seller_resources

Helpful Tool, BizBuySell Insight Reports; http://www.bizbuysell.com/news/media_insight.html

CHAPTER 2/SECTION 5

PREPARING A SELLING MEMO

Whether you're selling your business on your own or through a broker, you'll need to be ready to present a thorough written overview of your business and why it's a good purchase prospect.

Some brokers call this document a selling memo. Others call it a confidential description book or an offering memo.

- If your business is very small, uncomplicated, and likely to sell for under $200,000, you can probably reduce the selling memo to a terms sheet that presents little more than a business description, financial information, and presentation of price and terms.

- If your business is large, and if its assets, products and systems are complicated, your selling memo will likely run considerably longer in order to adequately explain your offering and its higher price.

This section outlines the contents for a complete selling memo, along with advice for how to distribute the information to prospective buyers and why and how to obtain confidentiality agreements beforehand.

Step-by-step actions

Step 1.   Prepare your selling memo.

Your selling memo is the first comprehensive description of your business that your prospective buyer will see. It needs to strike a careful balance between delivering facts about your business while also offering an inspiring description of its future potential.

- It presents facts about what your business is and does, and what makes it an attractive purchase opportunity without revealing sensitive information that you or your ultimate buyer won't want non-buyers (especially competitors) to know.

- It doesn't stretch the truth or overlook weaknesses, as you'll need to warrant the accuracy of all information you've provided before a sale closes.

- It shows earnings and asking price information without disclosing complete financial statements.

- It inspires buyers to take the next step by contacting you for more information.

The following chart lists information included in the selling memo for a business that aims to sell for a price over $200,000.

SELLING MEMO CONTENTS	✓
Table of Contents if memo is longer than 4-5 pages.	
Summary if memo is longer than 10 pages. (See Step 2.)	
Business Description --Summary of business history. --Business structure (sole proprietorship, partnership, corporation) and ownership. --Short description of products, staffing, markets and operations. --Financial information including annual sales and earnings; description of products/services; description of key strengths; reason for sale.	
Location Geographic location, building description, lease information.	
Business Strengths --List of business strengths and competitive advantages. --List of business challenges accompanied by statements of how the issue could be overcome or provide a growth opportunity.	
Competitive Overview --Description of number of competitors without listing names --Description of competitive position and advantages of your business	

SELLING MEMO CONTENTS	✓
Products/Services --Brief description of business offerings including product list. --Description of distinguishing product/service features. --Product sales trends.	
Operations --Information on operating hours and seasonality. --List of operating equipment. --Inventory information and list. --Production processes. --Staffing overview.	
Marketing --Industry information and growth trends. --Geographic information and growth trends. --Customer profile including information on client lists. --Description of competition and competitive rank. --Description of marketing approach, marketing plan and untapped marketing opportunities.	
Key Management and Employees --Key employee job titles, job descriptions, length of employment, compensation, benefits and credentials (but not names) including information on contracts.	
Future Plans/Growth Projections --List growth opportunities, along with the investment in time, financial resources and staff required.	

SELLING MEMO CONTENTS	✓
Potential Buyer Concerns --Issues, if any, that buyers might see as purchase barriers. --Statements describing business, marketing, or transition plans that ease or overcome each potential concern.	
Financial Information --Statement of accounting method: Accrual or cash basis. --Revenues, net income, and seller's discretionary earnings for past three years presented not as financial statements, but as one-line summaries.	
Offering Price and Terms --Asking price (example: ABC Company, a California Subchapter S Corporation with all shares held by the owner. Asking price is $XXX.XXX). --Contents of sale (example: Sale includes assets. Furnishings, fixtures, and equipment have a fair market value of $XXX,XXX, detailed in the Appendix. Inventory to be included at cost). --Terms, including whether seller-financing is available (example: Seller requires $XXX,XXX at closing and the balance financed by SBA note or seller financing to qualified buyer at X percent over X years). --Buyer qualifications, if any. --Seller's timeframe including sale timeline and seller's willingness to remain during a transition period. --Statement of seller's willingness to sign a non-compete agreement.	

SELLING MEMO CONTENTS	✓
Appendix	
--Statement of seller's discretionary earnings.	
--Financial statements as recommended by broker and accountant.	
--Asset list showing values.	
--Seller's disclosure statement, prepared with assistance from broker or attorney, providing an accurate assessment of business condition, a list of licenses and regulations that apply, and descriptions of any legal issues.	
--Market area information if business relies on local clientele.	
--Photos of business location, building and equipment.	
--Copies of marketing materials.	

Step 2. Create a summary of your selling memo to use during early communications with prospective buyers.

If your selling memo runs many pages long, as a first step present only the memo's summary that includes the following information:

- Business name, owner's name, and contact information.

- Business description, as in the selling memo.

- An overview of business strengths, competitive position, financial performance.

- Offering price and terms, as in the selling memo.

Step 3. Create a plan for sharing your selling memo and summary.

Consider the following approach:

- When you receive inquiries from business-for-sale ads, don't send your full selling memo if it is long and provides a detailed description of your business. Instead, respond with a copy of your selling memo summary. This allows you time to further assess the buyer's interest and financial capability before sharing further details.

- Share your selling memo or summary only with prospective buyers you deem – based upon the information they've provided – to be qualified prospects, and never before obtaining a signed confidentiality agreement, covered in the next step. Chapter 3 provides advice on how to pre-qualify prospects.

Step 4. Be ready to obtain confidentiality agreements before releasing your selling memo.

- Buyers understand they'll need to sign confidentiality or non-disclosure agreements before receiving information on businesses for sale, so be ready and don't be hesitant about asking.

- Use a form provided by your broker or attorney or one you can download from the BizBuySell site, listed in the Resources section of this page. Chapter 4/Section 2 lists steps to follow when screening and qualifying potential buyers, including when to obtain confidentiality agreements before sharing information. At this point, you just want to be prepared by having the forms ready to use.

Resources:

The book, *Selling Your Business for Dummies*, Chapter 8, describes the contents of a selling memo in detail. The book's CD-ROM also includes a selling memo template.

Article, *Keeping it Confidential;* http://www.bizbuysell.com/seller_resources

Article, *Documents and Information Required for Selling a Business;* http://www.bizbuysell.com/seller_resources;

Buyer Confidentiality Agreement Sample Form http://www.bizbuysell.com/fsbo/resources/restricted/buyer-confidentiality-agreement.pdf

CHAPTER 2/CONCLUSION

Congratulations! You've now concluded the second chapter in the BizBuySell Guide to Selling Your Small Business.

In Section 1 you created a list of all the actions necessary before offering your business for sale

In Section 2 you began the process of assembling the documents you'll need throughout the sale process

In Section 3 you started making decisions about who will be on your business sale team

In Section 4 you tackled the big issue of pricing your business

In Section 5 you learned what needs to go into the selling memo you'll provide to qualified buyers after they pledge to keep the information confidential

Now you're ready to prepare for launch your business-for-sale marketing process, which is the topic of Chapter 3 and the next section in this guide.

CHAPTER 3

MARKETING YOUR BUSINESS FOR SALE

Overview

You're ready to launch the business-for-sale marketing process once you've taken these steps:

- You've set your goals and objectives and are clear about what you want out of the sale of your business. (if not, see Chapter 1)

- Your business is prepped and ready to attract buyers (Chapter 2 will help you through this process).

Now it's time to start attracting buyers.

This chapter describes what goes into marketing your business, from developing a target-buyer description to planning how you'll choose marketing channels, create and place ads, and prepare to keep the whole process confidential in order to protect the ongoing operation of your business from disruption.

In four sections, Chapter 3 covers:

1. Protecting confidentiality while marketing your business for sale
2. Understanding and choosing marketing options
3. Writing ads that attract and pre-qualify buyers
4. Creating compelling online ads

Count on this chapter to guide you through the steps involved to get your offering in front of prospective buyers.

Key terms in this chapter:

Online Business-for-Sale Sites: High-traffic sites where you or your broker, if you're using one, will post your for-sale ad to reach the hundreds of thousands of buyer prospects who begin their searches online. The biggest online sites are bizbuysell.com and bizquest.com.

Blind Ad: An ad in which your business identity isn't revealed. Responses are directed to a media-provided address or to an email address you establish specifically to collect inquiries without divulging your business name until you pre-qualify the prospects as capable and qualified to buy your business.

Confidentiality Agreement: A written legal document signed by two or more parties who agree not to reveal sensitive information obtained during private discussions; a necessary form to obtain before identifying your business to a prospective buyer (also called a Non-Disclosure Agreement). If signed by both you and your prospective buyer, it is called a Mutual Confidentiality Agreement.

Warranties and Representations: A statement in a buyer's purchase offer and contract that requires you to warrant or guarantee that your business is in the condition you've represented and that facts you've presented are accurate to the best of your knowledge. From the first ad through to the day of closing be careful to share information that is absolutely true. Should a buyer learn otherwise, your sale can be jeopardized and the buyer can seek recourse.

CHAPTER 3/SECTION I

PROTECTING CONFIDENTIALITY WHILE MARKETING YOUR BUSINESS FOR SALE

Once you start marketing your business, your business sale will be about all you can think about. Here's some important advice: As much as possible, keep your thoughts to yourself.

Confidentiality is generally needed during the selling process.

It's important for reaching your own exit goals. And it's important for the success of your business after-the-sale, especially if you provide seller financing and agree to receive some of the purchase price in the form of future payments from the buyer.

Letting the word leak out prematurely is harmful in a number of ways:

- Customers, competitors, creditors and employees become hesitant when a business is for sale, often triggering reactions that can weaken your business momentum and therefore its value.

- Prospective buyers become hesitant about purchasing a business if they feel sensitive information has been divulged to others.

- Telling even close confidants can launch an unintentional gossip chain. If each person tells only one other trusted friend or relative, news of your sale intentions can spread far and quickly, especially if word gets out among competitors, employees, or others in your industry.

There are some less common situations when confidentiality may not be important or could even be a hindrance to maximizing the sale price, so you will have to use your own judgement on which scenario applies to your situation or not.

Some different scenarios when confidentiality may not be needed:

- If your business is located in a rural market, and your business is the only business operating in a certain category.

- Your business is very well-known and respected in its local market (certain retail businesses may fit this, and you want widespread knowledge that your brand is for sale)

- A fire sale scenario (owner has suddenly died and business is not operating)

- When selling to employees, to a partner, or family member.

This section is one of the longest in the *BizBuySell Guide to Selling Your Small Business* because the topic of confidentiality is so important to a successful sale. To protect your business and your sale hopes, take the following actions.

Step-by-step actions

Step 1. Advertise your business using blind ads and listings.

Don't share your personal or business name until you've qualified prospective buyers and obtained their confidentiality commitments. And certainly don't announce your name in for-sale ads.

Advertise the nature and strength of your business instead of its name. For example: PROFITABLE PALM SPRINGS FLORIST WITH LONG-TERM ESTABLISHED CUSTOMER BASE FOR SALE.

Direct responses to an address that doesn't reveal your personal or business identity. When placing ads in traditional media, use media-provided P.O. Box or e-mail options that allow you to maintain confidentiality and, – a big time-saving bonus – to follow up only with prospects you decide are qualified to buy your business. When using online business-for-sale sites, use the sites' identity-protecting features. Buyers on the BizBuySell site click a reply button that reads, "Contact the seller," which allows you to obtain initial responses without revealing the name of your business. Chapter 3/

Section 1 provides information on obtaining a confidentiality or non-disclosure agreement before sharing further information. Sections 3 & 4 in this chapter provide detailed advice for creating your sale-offering ads.

Step 2. Pre-qualify buyers before sharing sensitive information.

If you feel awkward about asking a prospective buyer for financial and business background information before divulging your business name, you're not alone. But realize this:

- Qualified buyers expect you to screen out other buyers before sharing sensitive information.

- Qualified buyers care about the privacy of your business information because they want to know that the business they're buying has carefully protected its trade secrets and financial information.

- Qualified buyers are serious shoppers and they're ready with the information necessary to take the next steps.

According to business brokers, nine out of ten respondents to business-for-sale ads aren't qualified to make the purchase. That's why pre-qualification is so important. The sooner you learn who can and can't buy your business, the better – both for you and for your ultimate buyer.

An effective way to pre-qualify prospects is to describe your business and response requirements in a way that helps unqualified buyers opt themselves out.

By describing the size of your business and your purchase price, and then by asking interested parties to respond by describing their purchase capabilities, you stand a good chance of hearing only from those who, in fact, are qualified to buy your business.

In every ad you place, in print or online, ask interested parties to respond with information that describes:

- What they're seeking from a business purchase
- Their purchase timeline

- A description of their related business experience
- Their interest in and ability to buy your business

You can cover this request in one sentence: Please respond describing your related business background, the type and size business you seek, your investment capability and your interest in this business.

Step 3. Create an inquiry response system that shares information confidentially and in phases.

You don't need to tell a buyer everything at once. In fact, revealing too much information in your ads can give away your identity even when you're careful not to share your business name.

The following chart provides an example of when and how to phase your information delivery.

Delivery Stage	Included Information	Confidentiality Request
Business-for-sale ads	Brief description of business type, strength, size and price.	Online listing can be set up to request confidentiality. Example: "Before releasing further details, the party offering this business for sale requires a signed confidentiality agreement. Click to view and print the form."
	Request for interested parties to respond by describing purchase intentions and qualifications.	
	Request for responses to a blind P.O. Box, email address, or media collection point that doesn't reveal your business or personal name.	Brokers require interested parties to provide financial capability and non-disclosure agreements before receiving additional information.

Delivery Stage	Included Information	Confidentiality Request
Phone or email replies to qualified ad respondents	Personal introduction and additional information that doesn't reveal sensitive information or business name.	Share additional business information only in return for buyer information and only in general terms.
	Probe/confirm interest, financial capability, purchase interests, timeline.	
	Offer to email or fax your brief selling memo summary (see Chapter 2/ Section 5) but with any references to your business identity removed.	
	If interest and capability is high, request a personal meeting before sharing more information.	
Initial personal meeting, held in person unless distance requires a phone meeting.	Reconfirm prospect interest and capability. After guaranteeing confidentiality, share your selling memo to be read during the meeting.	Meet off-site to protect identity of your business – likely in your broker's, accountant's or attorney's office. Reconfirm serious interest and request signatures on a mutual confidentiality agreement prepared or reviewed in advance by your attorney.

Delivery Stage	Included Information	Confidentiality Request
Delivery of selling memo	See Chapter 2/Section 5 for a complete list of selling memo contents.	Share selling memo only after receiving a signed confidentiality agreement and only to be read during the meeting unless you're extremely confident about the buyer's interest/capability. Otherwise, release only the memo summary.
Due Diligence	Reveal financial records and business operations.	Reveal only after receiving the buyer's formal letter of intent to purchase your business.
	Release a copy of your selling memo, with each page numbered (#1, for example) so they can be traced to the buyer's copy should they later be copied or circulated.	

Step 4. Prepare for maintaining confidentiality.

To maintain privacy throughout the selling process, take these steps:

Have a confidentiality agreement ready for presentation to serious, qualified buyers. Use our sample provided on the following page , a sample that your broker (if you use one) provides, purchase one from a form shop or site, or work with your attorney, who should review the form you plan to use even if he or she doesn't produce it for you. Be sure to include a clause that ensures mutual confidentiality and an expiration date that allows the confidentiality assurance to expire, usually after two years.

Establish a private email account for use exclusively with prospective buyers. Otherwise, you risk tipping off employees and causing concern within your business. Instead, invite buyers to send a confidential email to a non-business address, which you set up exclusively for the purpose of business sale communications. Don't use your personal name, as it's too easily traceable, but rather create an address that disguises who you are. For example, landscapingoffer@gmail.com or even a line-up of random letters and numbers.

Direct calls to a non-business phone number, and be sure to answer the phone or offer a voicemail message that conveys appropriate greetings to business buyers. Keep in mind that your home phone may not be appropriate here, as employees, vendors or competitors who know you personally might recognize your phone number or your identity on your answering machine.

Even with a signed confidentiality agreement, until you have a letter of intent or a buyer's offer in hand, don't share proprietary processes, trade secrets, client lists, or financial details about your business. Your sale offering likely listed annual revenues and owner's cash flow, along with asking price. Don't share further financial details until the prospective buyer has demonstrated clear ability to purchase and pledged to maintain confidentiality.

Be prepared for questions from employees and associates, who may suspect your sale intentions. You can be truthful without spilling the beans. You can say you're developing an exit plan to ensure future stability for your business; you can say you're talking to potential partners or successors without out-and-out announcing they'll be replacing you near-term. If people ask, "Are you thinking about selling," you can follow the suggestion of Appraiser Glen Cooper and answer, "Sure, I'll always talk to someone who wants to buy me out! Did you bring your check book?"

Resources:

Article, *Confidentiality Breach Can Ruin a Business Sale*; http://www.gaebler.com/confidentiality-breach-can-ruin-business-sale.htm

Sample Form, Buyer Confidentiality Agreement; http://www.bizbuysell.com/fsbo/resources/restricted/buyer-confidentiality-agreement.pdf

CHAPTER 3/SECTION 2

UNDERSTANDING AND CHOOSING YOUR MARKETING OPTIONS

The most frequently asked question from those selling small businesses has to do with where and how to find buyers.

Small businesses are used to bootstrapping and implementing guerrilla tactics, and therefore they're used to getting the word out via networking, flyers, even signs in windows – none of which works well in the business sale process.

As the preceding section in this chapter explained, this is a time for discretion and confidentiality.

You need to offer your business for sale in a manner that doesn't tip off customers, creditors or employees. And most certainly you don't want to let competitors know your sale plans – unless you're considering a specific competitor as a likely buyer.

If you know a specific person or business that's likely to buy your business, you can proceed with a confidential inquiry. To cast more widely for buyers, the only safe approach is to offer your business for sale discreetly and without identification, using brokers or blind ads to get the word out.

The following steps help you sort through and decide on your options.

Step 1: Define the likely buyer of your business.

Remember the old line, "Fish where the fish are biting"? In some ways, deciding where to advertise your business follows that age-old advice. Figure out who is most likely to buy your business, and then think about where and how you can best reach your prospects.

- Is your business likely to sell to someone seeking to buy *any* business or a business specifically like yours?

- Can *anyone* who is financially qualified buy your business or does the buyer need to have specific qualifications, credentials, or licenses?

- Do you think your business is most apt to sell to an individual buyer, or to another business, or to an investor group?

Step 2: Determine how best to reach the likely buyer of your business.

The following chart helps you zero in on the person or business most likely to acquire your business, along with the marketing approaches most likely to reach the buyer you've defined.

BUYER PROFILE			
	Marketing Approach		
Buyer Description	Local ads; local broker	Industry-specific ads; industry-specific broker	Online business-for-sale sites	Confidential Inquiries
An individual who lives or wants to live in the region where your business is located, who is considering a wide range of business offerings specifically in your market area.*	✓		✓	
An individual who is considering a wide range of businesses in a number of geographic areas			✓	

BUYER PROFILE				
An individual or business seeking to acquire a business specifically of your type but in a number of geographic areas.		✓	✓	
An individual seeking a business of your type who has the specific credentials or certification to acquire your business.		✓	✓	✓
An investor or investor group seeking to acquire a business of your type in a number of geographic areas.		✓		✓
A competitor or supplier with a strategic reason to acquire your business				✓
An individual seeking to acquire a franchised business.	If you're selling a franchise, called a franchise resale, consult with your franchisor before beginning the sale process, both because there are contractual obligations to follow and because the franchisor may have a list of interested buyers to share. If not, use online listing sites through which you'll reach the broadest range of prospective buyers.			

When the buyer and seller are in the same market area the sale is called an "intramarket transaction," which describes the majority of all small business sales. Often these deals include a local broker, and almost always they involve online business-for-sale searches. Just as people search online for real estate in their own market areas, they also search the Internet for businesses for sale in their communities.

Step 3. Target your advertising efforts.

If you're using a broker to sell your business, the marketing of your business becomes the broker's responsibility. Still, it's worth it to understand where buyers are looking for businesses so you're in a good position to evaluate your broker's marketing plan or, if you're selling without an intermediary, to reach buyers on your own.

Match your likely buyer to one or several of the following descriptions to determine how best to reach your target audience.

- **Buyers interested only in business offerings in a specific market area** often work through local brokers. They also read local classified ads, and almost all search online listing sites, where they limit their searches to their desired market area. Many also ask bankers, accountants, attorneys or business leaders for leads, which you can tap into through very discreet networking, often working through the confidential relationship established with your accountant or attorney.

- **Buyers interested only in business offerings in a specific industry or professional arena** most likely search online listing sites where they can customize their searches by business type, size, and location. They also read trade publications and sites. Most also network to seek leads, which you can cultivate by making confidential contacts with association executives in your industry or professional arena.

- **Buyers interested in a wide range of businesses over a far-flung area** almost certainly search online business-for-sale sites for opportunities.

- **Nine out of ten prospective buyers shop online listings,** regardless of whether they're working with a broker, whether they're looking for businesses in a specific region or business arena, or whether they're open to a wide range of business and geographic areas.

CHAPTER 3/SECTION 3

WRITING ADS THAT ATTRACT AND PRE-QUALIFY BUYERS

Writing business-for-sale ads is an exercise in fine balance.

- You have to entice prospective buyers about the current and potential strength of your business without even slightly stretching facts, which you'll have to warrant as accurate at the time of an actual purchase.

- You have to tell enough about your business to make buyers think they'd like to know more but you can't tell so much that readers – particularly competitors – can piece together the facts into a description of your business.

- You have to keep ads short yet build enough interest and trust to prompt prospective buyers not just to respond but to respond with information about their financial and business capability to make a purchase.

- You have to indicate enough about your business size and price to attract interest from those qualified to make the purchase while allowing those who don't match up with your asking price to rule themselves out.

- And maybe most importantly, you have to make your business stand out from the crowd of other businesses listed in the same place, whether it is on an online business-for-sale marketplace, a classified ad, or an ad in a trade publication.

It's a tall order.

This section provides information on what to know and what to do as you develop your business-for-sale ads. The following section in this chapter deals specifically with how to master the art of online ads.

Step-by-Step actions

Step 1. Provide a concise yet thorough description of your business offering.

In a matter of sentences, your ad needs to provide an overview of what your business is and why it's an attractive purchase opportunity, all without stretching the truth or presenting information you can't later warrant as true and accurate.

Here's what to convey:

What buyer wants to know	Advice to follow
What your business is and does	Be clear and specific. Instead of "Manufacturing Business" say "Manufacturer of low-tech product for high-tech industry." Instead of "Advertising Agency" say "Profitable 15-year advertising agency in growing metro area serving a roster of regional and national clients."

What buyer wants to know	Advice to follow
Where your business is located	If your business is in New York City, say so, but if it's in a small town with only a few other businesses that fit the description, stating your exact location may give away your identity and sale intentions. Especially online, buyers search for businesses by location, so you can't avoid the location issue altogether. If it's in a small town, give a general description of its location. Instead of "Columbus, Ohio," say, "Located in Ohio," or "Located in a vibrant Ohio college town."
How long you've been in business	Buyers want to know if your business is established. You can convey this information in your description (profitable 12-year old jazz bar) or in your statement of strengths (serving government and commercial contracts since 2002).
The strengths or attributes that make your business attractive	Chapter 2/Section 1 includes a chart for assessing business attributes. In your ads, feature your business's strengths. "Profitable and growing," "in highly desirable location," "strong earnings," "well-known, highly regarded business name," "loyal staff and clients," "strong online and social media presence," "good growth potential." Just be sure every adjective you use can stand up to scrutiny, as you'll need to warrant accuracy when signing a purchase offer.

What buyer wants to know	Advice to follow
Your asking price	Not everyone agrees about stating an asking price, feeling it might scare some buyers away. Most advisors agree, however, that the advantages outweigh the disadvantages. Consensus is: State your asking price and most recent annual revenues. For one thing, online buyers shop by price category; if your price is missing, your business won't appear in the results. For another, if you don't list a price, you risk inspiring inquiries from those without the capabilities to complete a deal of your size.
Why you're selling	While it's not required, a description of why you're selling often inspires trust and increases response rates. Keep in mind that some reasons are very understandable; i.e., "retirement" or "death in the family", while others will discourage buyer responses, i.e., "burned out", or "declining business."

Business sale advisors agree on one point above all others: The less specific the business description presented in your sale ad, the more your business looks like any other. Your job is to compress the facts and strengths into a short ad that makes a buyer want to know more. Certified Business Appraiser Glen Cooper gives this example:

"Manufacturer for Sale. Call Broker. 555-1212" will get a minimal response. Describing the business for sale as a "Manufacturer of low-tech product" will get a better response. "Manufacturer of low-tech product in high-tech market" will get the best response.

Bottom line: Adding details to an ad usually improves response.

Step 2. Don't give away your business identity.

Protect your business identity in two ways:

- Place **"blind ads"** that don't reveal your business name or address, and that camouflage your identity by describing attributes without revealing facts buyers (or competitors) can link specifically to your business. When advertising using online sites, these ads are called "blind listings." Using a broker also solves this problem, as brokers will market your business and have inquiries directed to their office.

- Use the **identity-protecting features on business-for-sale listing sites.** This allows you to direct buyers to click to "contact the seller," after which they're prompted to enter information required by your listing. For instance, on BizBuySell you can mention in your listing that there is a "confidentiality agreement required," followed by instructions on how to print and submit the required form. You can also set your inquiry-response screen to read, "The party offering this business for sale asks you to please include the following information," followed by such specific requests as the buyer's preferred timeframe and investment capability.

Step 3. Help buyers self-qualify themselves by providing clearly defined purchase requirements.

State the annual revenues of your business as a way to help buyers determine whether your business is too large or too small to match their interests. Likewise, state your asking price to allow buyers to match their financial capabilities with your offering before responding to your ad. Though it seems counter-intuitive to write ads that narrow the response pool, when it comes to sharing information about your business, the goal is to deal only with those most interested and capable of making the purchase.

Step 4: Request inquiry responses that allow you to pre-screen buyers.

Don't limit your response invitation to a simple statement such as "contact the seller for more information." Instead, request and require specific information from respondents, including:

- Why they're interested in purchasing a business like yours.

- Their approximate timeframe.

- Their business experience.

- Their financial capability.

Online sites allow you to require this information as part of your listing-response mechanism in your description of the business, and if you're using a broker, that person will pre-screen responses on your behalf. If you're placing your own ads, your email response instructions might read, "Thank you for your inquiry about my business. Please reply with a description of your business background, the type and size business you seek to acquire, when you plan to purchase a business, your investment capability, and your interest in this business." While you may turn off some potential buyers, it is most likely that serious buyers will understand your efforts and reply with the requested information.

Step 5. Include a means to track ad responses.

If you place business-for-sale ads in a number of outlets, be prepared to track which placements draw the greatest number of well-qualified responses. This will help you reword non-performing ads to better reflect the content of well-producing ads. Also, if the identical ad works better in one media outlet than another, the finding may help you decide to concentrate your efforts in the media outlet that performs best. When using newspaper ads and online listing sites you can collect responses through the media channel for easy tracking. Keep in mind that the average business takes 6-12 months to sell, from beginning to end, so you will likely be "renewing" your advertising. For this reason it will help to understand which advertising outlets have generated buyer inquiries and which have not.

Resources:

Article, *Keeping It Confidential*; http://www.bizbuysell.com/seller_resources

CHAPTER 3/SECTION 4

MASTERING THE ART OF ONLINE ADS

With nine out of ten prospective buyers shopping online for acquisition opportunities, about the only reason not to list your business with online sites is if you have a specific buyer in mind and you don't want to deal with other interested parties. For everyone else, here's what to know about how online ads work and what makes them work well, taken from BizBuySell's article, *Ten Commandments of a Successful Business-for-Sale Listing*.

1. Include key financials	Include annual revenue and annual cash flow or seller's discretionary earnings. Without this, it's difficult for a potential buyer to know if your business fits his/her lifestyle/income needs and investment capability. Also, if your business listing doesn't provide this information but other similar business listings do provide it, buyers will be much more likely to respond to competitive ads.
2. Include geographic location	While listing sites allow you to keep location information confidential, don't. Most buyers search locations at least to the county level, which your listing should reveal. If a buyer is searching for a florist in Dade County Florida and your business's location is confidential, they WILL NOT see your listing in their search results.

3. Include a strong headline	In any type of ad, most people read only the headline. And they read more only if the headline grabs their attention and inspires their interest. Write a headline that presents what's great about your business. Is it the location? The great business space? The distinct and highly desirable products or services? The strong brand name and reputation? Ask: What would make you want to buy your business? Write a headline that conveys your answer. Keep in mind that when buyers first see listing results during an internet search, they are often comparing the prices and headlines for several businesses that meet their search criteria. You want YOURS to stand out.
4. Present the right contact information	Buyers want to see a phone number, but to protect your business identity, don't present your business phone number or a personal number. Direct calls to your broker's number, if you're using one, or to an unlisted number that can't be traced to you personally or to your business. Also, offer an email address that reaches an account you establish specifically for sale purposes. This separate email account will protect your established accounts from spam, maintain confidentiality, and make monitoring ad responses quick and easy. Then commit to checking for responses frequently and responding promptly (within a day or two maximum). The quickest way to kill buyer interest is with lack of response.
5. List your business in two categories	Most online listing sites allow you to select a "best matching business type" and a "next best-matching business type." For maximum exposure, choose a category for each option. For instance, "Gas Stations/Service Stations" and "Auto Service/ Repair".

6. Be descriptive and specific	Section 3 in this chapter provides a list of information your ad should cover. This isn't the time to be stingy with details. You can't turn your ad into a novel, but in short statements you need to describe your business, its history and its strengths, in enough detail to cause buyers to think you have nothing to hide and much to like. This is your chance to differentiate your business from the others that the buyer might consider. Don't spare words and risk losing them at the starting gate.
7. Include pictures	Without revealing your business identity, present photos that convey the quality of your business interior, equipment, or other aspects that will heighten buyer interest and confidence. At a minimum, if you can't include a photo that doesn't give away the identity of your business, include a generic photo to catch the buyer's eye. For example, if you're selling an Italian Restaurant, a nice photo of a classy looking dish of spaghetti and meatballs should be enough to draw the searcher's eye to your listing.
8. Retain confidentiality	Without revealing your business identity, provide as much information about your business and its location to prompt buyer interest. Disclose your state and county without telling your city (if it's small and you're one of few businesses that match your description) or address. Instead, provide general information, "near major highway," "one of the town's busiest streets," "one of the leading players in the industry."

9. Upgrade your listing if doing so will improve responses	Especially if your business is of high-value and of interest to only a narrow buyer segment, consider investing in what's called a "showcase ad," which places your listing above others, sends it via email to potential buyers who match your buyer criteria, and provides you with a prospect list for personal follow-up. If you're uncertain about the benefit, start with the basic ad and then consider upgrading if you aren't happy with the response.
10. Proofread	There's nothing like a typo-riddled ad to send buyer interest (and price offers) southbound. It's your sole responsibility to double check the text you provide to listing sites. Use spell check, proofread it yourself, and then give it to a trusted, confidential advisor for a final review before releasing it for online posting.

CHAPTER 3/CONCLUSION

Congratulations! You've now concluded the third chapter in the BizBuySell Guide to Selling Your Small Business.

- In Section 1 you prepared for the actions necessary to maintain confidentiality through the business-for-sale process.

- In Section 2 you sorted through and chose among the options for marketing your business to prospective buyers.

- In Section 3 you determined what goes into (and what stays out of) a great business-for-sale ad.

- In Section 4 you learned the Ten Commandments for online listings.

Now you're ready to prepare for the actual selling process, beginning with the important task of collecting, screening and communicating with prospective buyers before meeting in person, showing your business, conducting due diligence, and receiving and negotiating a purchase offer, all of which is explained in the upcoming Chapter 4.

CHAPTER 4

THE SELLING PROCESS

Overview

This is the point where your sale intentions launch into the high-gear effort of actually meeting and negotiating with your prospective buyer. So far, you've taken these steps:

- You've set your goals and objectives and are clear about what you want out of the sale of your business. (If not, see Chapter 1).

- Your business is prepped and ready to attract buyers (Chapter 2 will help you through this phase).

- Your ads are placed and inquiries are coming in (for advice on this phase, see Chapter 3).

Now it's time to start screening and meeting with prospective buyers to confirm interest and financial capability, present your business, conduct the due diligence process, and negotiate the many fine points involved in actually selling your business to a new owner.

This chapter describes what to expect, how to proceed, and what steps to take to keep buyer enthusiasm high, while also protecting your own interests as you move toward the selling finish line.

In five sections, Chapter 4 covers:

1. An overview of the selling process and the timeline it involves
2. Screening and communicating with buyers
3. Showing your business and building buyer trust
4. Receiving and negotiating a purchase offer
5. Conducting due diligence

Count on this chapter to guide you through the steps involved as you meet and negotiate with the buyer of your business.

Key terms in this chapter:

Due Diligence: The process of research and investigation that proceeds a purchase, during which time a buyer seeks to fully understand the condition of your business through a review of all financial records and obligations such as debts, pending or potential legal issues, leases, warranties, long-term customer agreements, employment contracts, compensation agreements, supplier and distributor agreements, and more. Simultaneously, as the seller, you perform a due diligence review to confirm the buyer's ability to purchase and run your business, particularly if part of the purchase price is in the form of a seller-financed loan of deferred payments and earn outs.

Letter of Intent to Purchase: A document presenting the buyer's proposed offer including price, sale structure, payment terms, and conditions involved to purchase your business. Creation of the letter is the buyer's obligation. The letter is not a binding legal document but it forms the basis for all future discussions and negotiations that culminate in the final deal and sale closing. Once signed by both parties, the letter of intent signifies mutual interest to complete the business sale transaction.

Earnest Money: A deposit sometimes requested by sellers at the time a buyer's purchase offer is received. Instead of earnest money, brokers usually collect 10 percent of the purchase price upon receipt of a purchase offer. The deposit or earnest money is held in an escrow account until sale closing.

Asset Sale: The most common form of small business sale, in which the seller keeps the actual, legal business structure, called the business entity, and sells only tangible and intangible business assets, which the buyer moves into a newly formed business entity. An asset sale is the only sale approach for sole proprietorships, which have no stock to sell.

Entity Sale: Also called a *stock sale.* A sale in which the owner of a corporation sells its stock or the owner of an LLC sells its membership shares. With the sale of stock or membership sales, the seller transfers all business assets and liabilities that aren't specifically excluded. As a result, an entity sale often results in a lengthier and more complicated due diligence process than is the case with a sale involving only clearly itemized assets.

Sale Structure: Generally refers to the legal manner, in which a business is sold, either as an asset sale or an entity sale.

Payment Structure: A factor in all but the rare few sales that are paid off on closing day. The payment structure involves the details of how the purchase price will be paid. In small business sales, payments usually take the form of a sizable down payment at closing followed by deferred payments in the form of seller-financed loan payments, balloon payments, or earn out payments.

Price Allocation: A determination agreed upon by the buyer and seller, with advice from accountants and attorneys, for how the purchase price will be spread across seven IRS-determined asset classes. How the price is allocated affects how the buyer's payments can be expensed and how the seller's receipts will be taxed, which often makes price allocation a matter of negotiation, since the buyer and seller must both report the same price allocation to the IRS, using Form 8594.

CHAPTER 4/SECTION I

THE SELLING PROCESS AND THE TIMELINE IT INVOLVES

Up to this point, you could manage your sale timeline pretty much on your own terms. Based purely on your own schedule, you could decide when to start the process, when and how to prepare your business, and when to start advertising to reach prospective buyers.

But the minute the first prospective buyer responds to one of your ads, the days of taking action on your own terms are over.

Simply put, time delays kill the enthusiasm of prospective buyers.

This section details what's involved in the buyer-seller communication and negotiation process, how long most sales take, and why immediate, focused response is critical from here on out.

Step-by-step actions

Step I.   Get clear about the timeframe of typical small business sales.

Even with the most efficient and effective communications, be prepared for your business sale transaction to take time.

- If you've got a buyer ready and waiting for you to say, "let's make a deal," your sale could sail through in a matter of months. That's a best-case scenario.

- If you're holding out for an extraordinarily high price – especially if your business isn't highly attractive and with strong future potential – expect your sale efforts to stretch out for a long, long time. In between are all the other deals. Surveys of business brokers show that most sales take at least 6-12 months to close, with at least ten percent of deals taking even longer. And of course, not all businesses sell. Unreasonable prices, all-cash demands, unattractive business conditions, and lack of financial, asset and inventory documentation can all contribute to a lack of buyer interest.

Step 2. Be ready to steer through the following give-and-take negotiations.

Here's an illustration of the buyer-seller interactions you're about to navigate.

Buyer Responds to Ad ➜ *Based on Preliminary Pre-Screening Buyer Appears Qualified* ➜ You Contact Buyer Without Revealing Your Business Identity ➜ *Based on Buyer's Response to Further Inquiry, Buyer Appears Capable of a Purchase* ➜ You Meet with Buyer in Location that Doesn't Reveal Your Business Identity ➜ *Buyer Remains Interested; Signs Confidentiality Agreement* ➜ You Identify Your Business and Present Your Selling Memo ➜ *Buyer Remains Interested* ➜ Buyer Tours Business; Discusses Offering ➜ Buyer Presents Letter of Intent to Purchase ➜ *You and Buyer Agree on Offer or Counter-Offer* ➜ You and Buyer Conduct Due Diligence ➜ You and Buyer Negotiate Sale Structure and Payment Structure ➜ You and Buyer Sign Purchase and Sale Agreement ➜ SALE CLOSING!

Step 3. Know the bailout points.

In the illustration shown in Step 2, each interaction that's *italicized* indicates a decision point.

At each decision point, you need to make an assessment about the buyer's business qualifications, financial capability, purchase interest, and willingness to negotiate a mutually acceptable deal.

If at any point you believe – based on documentation the buyer has provided or information the buyer has communicated – that the buyer is unqualified, incapable, disinterested, or unwilling to negotiate, be prepared to politely end interactions. This call is entirely up to you as the seller; you don't have to interact with, or sell to, anyone who you are not comfortable dealing with.

The following sections in this chapter provide advice for assessing the likelihood that a buyer's interest will result in a purchase, along with approaches for overcoming hesitations if possible – or ending interactions if necessary.

CHAPTER 4/SECTION 2

SCREENING AND COMMUNICATING WITH BUYERS

The first decision in the process of dealing with buyers involves screening inquiries from those who respond to your business-for-sale ads. Be prepared: Most sale advisors will tell you that nine out of ten people who respond to sale ads never make a purchase. They'll also tell you that a good many of those who do respond simply don't have the qualifications or capabilities to buy the business being offered.

- **Some are wannabe shoppers** who want to buy a business but are in no way ready to do so right now because they either lack the financial resources or business acumen to complete a purchase.

- **Some are tire-kickers** who are simply curious about what kinds of opportunities are out there.

- **Some are competitors** masquerading as buyers in order to gather intelligence.

- **Some are what those in the industry call "sharks"** who are searching for sellers who look overly anxious to sell and who may be willing to accept rock-bottom prices.

Your job, or your broker's job if you're using one, is to separate the strong bets from all the others.

Step-by-step actions

Step 1. Be clear about the necessary attributes of your likely buyer. Screening ad responses gets easy only if you know your knockout factors. So make a list of what qualifications and capabilities are essential:

- What business experience, professional certifications, etc., are absolutely necessary?

- How much cash do you think you'll require on closing day?

- If you'll be offering a seller-financed loan, what type and level of solid collateral will you require as security?

- What timeframe must the buyer be prepared to act within?

Step 2. Screen and sort ad respondents by their ability and likelihood to buy your business.

Following the steps in Chapter 3/Section 3 and Chapter 3/Section 4, your ads will provide information to help unqualified buyers opt themselves out, plus they'll require respondents to provide information that allows you to pre-screen their capabilities before pursuing their interest further. Based on the information each prospective buyer submits, complete the following pre-qualification form:

Qualifying questions:	Yes	Maybe	No
Is the buyer specifically interested in your business or market area?			
Does the buyer possess the necessary education, licenses, certifications or experience?			
Is the buyer interested in making a purchase within your timeframe?			
Is the buyer seeking a business of your size and in your price range?			
Does the buyer have the ability to meet your closing day payment expectations?			
Is the buyer qualified for an SBA or other third-party loan (or to meet your seller-financed loan qualifications)?			

- If a prospective buyer earns a line-up of "yes" answers, you know you have a solid lead.

- A string of "no" answers lands an inquiry in the "not now/maybe never" pile.

- Those who get "maybe" answers need to share additional information about their qualifications before you can screen them in or out as prospective buyers.

Step 3.   Verify the information the buyer has provided.

If you're working with a broker, that person will handle the task of obtaining information that verifies the buyer's financial capability, business licenses or certifications, or other necessary qualifications.

If you're working without a broker, you'll need to verify facts on your own, probably with help from your accountant and attorney. This involves requesting copies of bank statements, financial statements, professional licenses and certificates, and other documentation.

Qualified, serious buyers will be prepared for such requests, though often they'll feel comfortable releasing information only after signing mutual non-disclosure or confidentiality agreements (see Chapter 3/Section 1 for information on this topic) and only as part of a trust-building quid pro quo exchange during which you release facts and financial information about your business in exchange for similar information from the buyer, as detailed in the upcoming steps in this section and chapter.

Step 4.   Immediately follow up with hot leads.

When a buyer appears uniquely qualified, financially capable, and a good match with your business offering and sale timeline, issue an immediate response.

1. Pick up the phone.	Identify yourself if your name isn't likely to reveal your business identity. Otherwise, say you're the owner of the business the buyer inquired about. Convey your thanks for the inquiry and your preliminary belief in the buyer's suitability with your offer.
2. Confirm and deepen your impression about the buyer's qualifications and capabilities	Without revealing your business identity, establish rapport through a conversation that provides and obtains information in an answer-to-answer trade off. If you want to learn more about the buyer's cash condition, offer some financial information first. For example, roughly describe your business size before explaining that the sale offering requires $XX,XXX cash down at closing. This gives the buyer some information before requesting information in return. *Expect as many as half of respondents to drop out at this point. Either they won't have the money or experience to continue discussions. Better to learn that now than later.*
3. Email or fax your selling memo summary.	If you believe the buyer is an able and likely buyer, share your selling memo summary – but with all identifying information deleted.

4. Schedule a meeting.	Keep your business identity confidential by meeting off premise, preferably in the office of your accountant or attorney. Explain that you'll begin the meeting by signing a mutual confidentiality agreement (see Chapter 3/Section 1) after which you'll be able to share specific facts about your business.
	--If the buyer wants his or her accountant or attorney to attend this first meeting, welcome the additional attendees as a demonstration of the buyer's high interest.
	--If lack of proximity makes a personal meeting improbable, set up a phone meeting to be attended by you, the buyer and your accountant or attorney. Before the meeting, exchange confidentiality agreements.
	--If the buyer seems to need time before scheduling a meeting, offer to share the selling memo summary and to follow up in a day or two to schedule a meeting.

Step 5. Obtain additional information from possible but not-yet solid prospects.

If a prospective buyer appears somewhat qualified and capable to buy your business but you have reservations, hold off or get more information before sharing additional facts.

- **If you think the inquiry is from a competitor,** set the response aside unless you strongly believe that the competitor may be serious about purchasing your business. If so, proceed very cautiously, first by working to learn the prospect's identity and then by requiring a confidentiality agreement. Even with confidentiality assured, require the competitor to share the identical level of information about the competing business that you reveal about your own business.

- **If you have questions about the buyer's financial capability,** require information about how the buyer will finance a purchase before revealing any additional information. "Thank you for your interest in my business and sale offering. I look forward to providing more information. First, would you please reply with information about the size of business you're looking to acquire, your cash investment plans, and your ability to back a loan, if one is necessary, with collateral security?"

- **If you question the buyer's business qualifications,** move on *unless* your business requires no particular expertise *and* the buyer's financial condition is such that you'll be paid off on closing day. That's a rarity, for sure, but it will become a requirement if you sell your business to a person whose ability to run your business successfully is in question.

If you're using a broker, that person will handle pre-screening activity so you don't waste your time or divulge the sensitive facts about your business with those who aren't likely to buy. If you're not using a broker, it's your job to be sure you obtain the information necessary to answer the questions in the Step 1 chart with "yes" replies before revealing your business name, presenting your offering, and building the trust required for a buyer to make a purchase offer – all of which is the focus of the next section in this chapter.

CHAPTER 4/SECTION 3

SHOWING YOUR BUSINESS AND BUILDING BUYER TRUST

The minute you've established that a prospective buyer has high interest and high ability to buy your business, it's time to meet and begin serious discussions.

During the time immediately in front of you, it's still not the right time to bare the soul of your business. That will happen slowly and in phases, beginning with signatures on a confidentiality or non-disclosure agreement. Here's what to do, what to expect, and how to proceed during the steps you're about to take.

Step-by-step actions

Step 1. Host an initial meeting with the buyer.	Set the meeting without revealing your business identity. Meet in the office of your broker, if you're using one. If not, consider setting the meeting in your accountant's or attorney's office, possibly with your professional advisor or advisors present if your business sale is large or complex. (If location makes a face-to-face meeting impractical, conduct the meeting by phone.) If the buyer wants a professional advisor to attend as well, welcome the additional input as a demonstration of interest. Even if the buyer comes alone, however, simply by showing up, the buyer conveys a level of interest that speaks louder than words. It's your job to be sure the meeting isn't just cordial but that it actually advances the buyer-seller interaction.
	Reconfirm your initial impression about the buyer's interest and purchase ability. Restate the type and size of your business and your preliminary timeline. Also discuss the purchase structure in terms of the buyer's required cash investment and the need for solid security if you're considering making a seller-financed deal. Probe the buyer's reactions and input. The buyer likely received your selling memo summary (without business identification) before the meeting. Refer to that document while you reconfirm and deepen your confidence in the buyer's interest and purchase capability before moving on to the next step. *Otherwise, end discussions at this point by expressing thanks for the interest while explaining that the buyer's situation and your sale expectations appear not to match up.*

	Obtain the buyer's confidentiality agreement on a form your broker, if you're using one, or your attorney has reviewed and approved. Explain your need for agreement not to disclose confidential information obtained during upcoming discussions. *If the buyer doesn't pledge confidentiality, end discussions at this point.*
	Share your selling memo. Once the buyer has agreed to confidentiality and convinced you of serious intentions and ability to purchase, share but don't release your selling memo. Give the buyer time to review it carefully without allowing him or her to take it from the meeting – unless you are very confident of the buyer-seller match up and then only after numbering the memo and having the buyer initial every page. That way, if copies of pages end up in the wrong hands you can trace them back to the copy you gave the buyer. *If the buyer indicates reduced interest at this point, probe, address and overcome concerns or end discussions at this point.*
	Invite the buyer to tour your business. Before the initial meeting ends, schedule a tour of your business to keep interaction moving along.
Step 2. Present your business	Show your business only after inspecting and perfecting its physical condition, and during a time when it is active and impressive. For very small businesses where the tour may spark staff questions, consider an after-hours tour or be prepared to introduce the buyer as a colleague, associate or friend.
	Describe and point out features of your business and its strengths and opportunities. Conduct the same kind of tour you'd provide to an industry or community VIP, showing how a customer experiences your business before going behind the scenes to provide an overview of how your business works. Encourage and answer questions and learn more about the buyer's abilities and concerns. Share information without revealing trade secrets, proprietary processes, or any information that should be kept from anyone but the ultimate buyer of your business. *If the buyer indicates reduced interest at this point, probe, address and overcome concerns or end discussions at this point.*
	Follow the tour with a private meeting to address buyer questions. The buyer likely will ask: Why are you selling? Where are the problems? What's the potential? Be ready to address the buyer's interests discretely without revealing insider information. Also, don't negotiate price at this point. *If the buyer indicates reduced interest, probe, address and overcome concerns or end discussions at this point.*

	During the post-tour private meetings, learn more about the buyer. Learn whether the buyer has owned a business in the past; when the buyer is looking to complete a purchase, how long the buyer has been looking, how the buyer plans to fund a purchase, who else will be involved in the buyer's decision (for instance, a spouse, partner, banker or attorney). *If the buyer's answers cause you uncertainty about interest or capability, address and overcome concerns or end discussions at this point.*
	Schedule the next meeting. Following the meeting, the ball is in the buyer's court, but you'll want to keep the game moving. Schedule a follow-up meeting. Until that time, offer to provide information the buyer may have requested, such as marketing materials, product samples, or other information that cultivate interest without divulging inner-business workings. *If you sense that the buyer has lost interest or lacks the ability to pay the price you require (which is likely no less than 70 to 85 percent of your asking price), address and overcome issues or end discussions.*

As you take the steps outlined in this chart, remember at all times that your buyer wants and needs:

- A business that delivers immediate cash flow.

- A going concern with an established infrastructure.

- A strong financial condition backed by good historical data and financial statements.

- A broad-based, loyal, and transferable client base.

- A business that can be assumed with no transition hiccups.

As you interact with your prospective buyer address the above points, realizing that buyers pay a premium for businesses with upward-trending revenues and profits and good future opportunity.

At all times, however, take great care to truthfully convey facts about the condition of your business, because after you receive a purchase offer – which is the focus of the upcoming section – and before the sale can close, you'll have to warrant the accuracy of the information you've provided.

CHAPTER 4/SECTION 4

RECEIVING AND NEGOTIATING A PURCHASE OFFER

The whole point of your interactions with a prospective buyer is to prompt a purchase offer. You're not just doing this for fun, after all.

The purpose of this chapter is to help you move to the point where your buyer puts purchase intentions into writing and hands you – or your broker – a letter of intent to buy your business.

Here's what to do, what to expect, and how to proceed during the steps you're about to take.

Step 1. Obtain the buyer's letter of intent to purchase.

The letter of intent puts your buyer's proposal in writing.

If you're working with a broker, that person will receive and discuss the buyer's purchase intentions. Otherwise, the offer will come to you directly. When it does, if it comes in the form of a conversation, don't start talking price and terms. Instead, ask the buyer to detail price and terms in writing so you can respond thoughtfully with input from your accountant and attorney.

The "letter of intent" isn't a binding legal document, but it forms the basis for the all discussions leading up to a formal purchase offer. It will present the price, purchase structure, terms and purchase conditions your prospective buyer is proposing.

Step 2. Carefully review buyer's purchase proposal.

Happy as you'll be to receive a letter of intent; don't just sign on the dotted line. Too much is at stake. Instead, consult with sale advisors, including your broker, if you're using one, and your attorney and accountant. Discuss the following points:

The buyer's proposed price and payment structure	Most likely, the buyer will offer less than your asking price, which can become a point of later negotiation. The buyer also will describe how much will be paid in cash at closing and what kind of financing will be necessary. *Discuss the price and payment proposal with your accountant and attorney before discussing it with your buyer, because the payment structure will come with tax implications.*
The buyer's proposed purchase structure	The vast majority of small business sales are *"asset sales"* but a few are *"entity sales"*. The buyer will propose one or the other, likely based on the structure stated in your sale listing. *Your accountant and attorney will advise you on the ramifications of either structure for your sale and tax situation.*
The price allocation	The buyer may or may not describe a proposed approach for allocating the price, but be prepared for this important topic, which greatly affects how sale proceeds are taxed and upon which the IRS requires you and the buyer to agree. Obtain your accountant's advice before discussing or accepting proposals on this topic.
Purchase exclusions or additions	Proposed exclusions or additions to your sale offering can greatly affect your sale proceeds and how they're taxed, and they can also affect the liabilities you retain after the sale closes. *Get advice from your attorney or accountant before agreeing to variances.*

Due diligence	Most buyers who are purchasing only the assets of a small business can complete due diligence in less than a month. Businesses with real property or extensive physical assets, or those selling as entity sales, often take longer. *Be sure the letter of intent states a reasonable due diligence period and that it stipulates that no information obtained during this investigation will be shared beyond the buyer's purchase advisors without your express permission.*
Warranties and representations	You'll need to guarantee that the facts you've presented about your business condition are accurate. *Be sure your attorney reviews the warranties and representations clause, however, because you want to warrant accuracy to the best of your knowledge, but you don't want to warrant completeness, since there may be conditions of which you honestly aren't aware.*
Seller's future involvement	The buyer's proposal may stipulate your after-sale transition-period or ongoing involvement with the business. It may also require you to sign a "covenant not to compete" with the business for a period of time after the sale. *Work with your attorney or broker to review the timeframe for future involvement, as well as the timeframe constraints and geographic area defined by the non-competition proposal.*
Additional stipulations	Expect the buyer's proposal to state: --Whether you're required to run the business as usual during the closing period (or whether the buyer asks for major agreements/purchases be put on hold). --That the offer is nonbinding. --Cancellation options. --An exclusivity agreement that prevents you from considering competing offers during the due diligence period.

Step 3. Respond to the buyer's proposal.

Based on input and advice from your sale advisors, you'll either sign to accept the buyer's offer or you'll propose a counter offer.

As you respond to the buyer's letter of intent, remember this isn't the time to negotiate fine points. Your objective is gain agreement on the major elements of the buyer's proposal, including price, payment structure, exclusions or additions to the sale, timeframe, and your after-sale involvement.

Determining sale details will happen during the negotiation of final terms prior to drawing up the final purchase agreement and before the formal closing of the deal, all covered in Chapter 5.

At this point, however, if your primary sale requirements differ greatly from the buyer's purchase intentions, you'll want to propose a counter offer, just as you'd do when accepting a purchase offer on your home. Involve your broker or your accountant or attorney to provide input, to share objective criteria, to serve as sounding boards and safety valves, and to help you avoid unnecessary disputes as you undertake the first of your buyer-seller negotiations, which are described more fully in Chapter 5/Section 3.

Step 4. Accept the buyer's offer.

To accept the buyer's offer, you and the buyer will sign either the initial letter of intent or a version that reflects mutually agreed upon changes. Either way, once your signatures are on the line, the letter signifies agreement to a purchase offer. Here's what typically happens next:

- **Your broker, if you're using one, will collect a deposit** of, usually, 10 percent of the proposed purchase price, to be held in an escrow account.

- **If you're not using a broker,** you and your sale advisors will decide whether to require a deposit from the buyer. If so, the deposit is called earnest money. If earnest money is involved, once it's collected, it's held in a third-party escrow account until any conditions stipulated in the letter of intent are adequately addressed and the sale closes.

From this point, your sale moves into the due diligence stage, which is outlined in the upcoming section of this chapter. More work lies ahead, but for the moment, take a deep breath and realize you've successfully attracted an offer from a qualified buyer. Congratulations!

CHAPTER 4/SECTION 5

CONDUCTING DUE DILIGENCE

An easy definition of due diligence is "serious investigation".

In almost all sales, due diligence is a condition of the buyer's offer. Only after determining that your business conditions meet expectations – or that problem conditions have or will be satisfactorily addressed – will the buyer remove the due diligence contingency and close the deal.

During due diligence, as the seller you need to be ready on two fronts:

- You need to be prepared to provide access to all the information the buyer will want to examine.

- You'll want to be ready to simultaneously examine your buyer's financial condition and managerial experience, especially if you'll be carrying a seller-financed loan or agreeing to accept deferred payments for a portion of the purchase price.

Step-by-step actions

Step 1.   Assemble the documentation you'll need to provide.

Use the following checklist of information likely to be required during due diligence:

Description of Material Likely to be Requested During the Buyer's Due Diligence
Corporate or Schedule C tax returns for Past 2-3 years, allowing buyer to verify the revenues shown on financial statements.
Business financial statements for the current and past 2-3 years including income statements, balance sheets, current cash flow statement, each presented in formal, professionally reviewed reports following industry standards.

	Annual owner's cash flow or seller's discretionary earnings statement that recasts your most recent annual income statement to reflect revenues and all essential operating costs without extraordinary, one-time or discretionary expenditures, therefore accurately presenting how much money the business actually generates for the benefit of its owner.
	Financial trends and ratios including such information as revenue and profit growth trends.
	Accounts receivables/accounts payable lists.
	Inventory list including value.
	Major equipment and furnishings lists including value.
	Supporting financial information such as inventory turnover rate, receivables collection rate, and current or liquidity ratio.
	Current building lease including information on lease duration and transferability.
	Fixtures, furnishings and equipment list indicating all items included in the sale, along with photos of major items, titles confirming ownership, lease and maintenance agreements, and depreciation schedules from most recent tax return.
	Copies of contracts and agreements with employees, customers, suppliers, distributors and others.
	Intellectual property documentation for patents, trademarks and other items, each showing ownership by the business rather than by individuals.
	Management and operational documentation including procedural manuals, product and pricing lists, other reports and agreements.
	Staffing records including list of employees with hire dates, salaries, contracts, and benefit summaries; description of employee benefits plan, organization chart and employment policy manual.
	Client information including information on transferable databases.
	Supplier and distributor lists including relationship descriptions and agreements.
	Business and marketing plans or summary descriptions.
	Business formation documents.

Step 2. Keep your sale intentions confidential while helping the buyer examine your business.

Due diligence requires careful management on your part. The buyer will want to meet and interact with staff and business clients and suppliers before you're prepared to make your sale plans public, so be ready to introduce the buyer in a manner that doesn't set off questions or fuel rumors.

- **If necessary, consider revealing your sale intentions to a very few key managers** if you and the buyer require their help during due diligence. Seek an agreement with the buyer that these top-level employees will be offered bonus compensation for assisting in the sale process and transition. When sharing the news with these select staff members, stress the buyer's strong qualifications and positive plans for the future of your business. At the same time, convey the due diligence timeline and the importance of keeping the sale confidential during that period.

- **Your broker, if you're using one, or your accountant can be a key resource during due diligence.** Their offices can serve as a repository for the documents the buyer needs to access. They can also be the place where you and the buyer meet in order to reduce on-site presence and questions in your own business setting.

- **Confirm with the buyer how to contact you,** likely through the email address and phone number you established specifically for sale purposes. Your aim at this point isn't to keep your business identity confidential – as it was during the initial stages of your marketing effort – but rather to keep the buyer's interactions less visible to customers, vendors and staff members.

Step 3. Be prepared for the scope of the buyer's investigation.

The buyer will likely want to research and examine the following aspects of your business:

- **Financial condition,** looking beyond previously provided financial statements to assess financial management and growth potential.

- **Business operations,** including how easily your production and other processes will transfer, the nature and transferability of your client base, billing and collection procedures, details about your staffing and management, as well as your marketing plan, including current and proposed marketing efforts.

- **Legal issues,** including information on legal obligations or potential problems ranging from pending litigation, pension liabilities, claims, tax audits, zoning issues, and a wide range of other possible issues that your attorney can help you list and prepare to discuss.

Plan to devote significant time to assisting with the buyer's investigation. Plan also to invest in the services of your accountant and attorney, who will help you determine what information to divulge and how to protect confidentiality if (and likely when) the buyer requests sensitive financial or other information to be shared with third-party reviewers.

Step 4. During due diligence, further investigate the capabilities of your buyer.

Especially if you're accepting part of the purchase price through deferred payments, due diligence gives you one more chance to verify the ability of the buyer both to make payments and to run your business in a manner that assures its success.

- **Obtain the buyer's personal financial statement and credit report.** You can obtain this information through your broker, if you're using one, or on your own. Then ask your accountant to review the information to examine the buyer's financial strength.

- **Conduct an online search for the buyer's name** to uncover publicity items and facts the buyer might not have shared.

- **Ask for personal, financial an business references** you can contact in an effort to discover whether or not the buyer presents a management or loan risk. Confirm with the buyer how to introduce yourself (if mutually you decide not to reveal purchase intentions), perhaps by telling the reference you're conducting reference checks in regards to a top-level position with your business.

- **Interview the buyer regarding plans to dramatically alter your business,** including changing its location, product line, pricing and staffing. This information will help you determine whether you believe the business is likely to succeed, and therefore earn the money necessary to make deferred payments of the purchase price. (Chapter 5 includes specific information on how to protect yourself if you're self-financing part of the purchase price.) It will also help you determine whether the buyer's plans are consistent with the assurances you have recently given or are hoping to give your established staff and customers.

Step 5. **Be patient.**

The buyer's due diligence investigation can easily take a month, and longer if your sale involves the transfer of stock (and therefore all known and unknown liabilities) or if the assets being acquired are difficult to examine and evaluate. The due diligence timeframe will likely be pre-set in the buyer's letter of intent, so you'll know what to expect. Still, it may feel prolonged and the investigation may feel intrusive and tiring. But it's necessary to get you to the next stage, which includes final negotiations, sale closing, and the transfer of your business, which is the focus of the upcoming chapter in this guide.

Resources:

The book, *Selling Your Business for Dummies,* includes a chapter describing the due diligence and detailing how to prepare for and conduct each aspect of the investigation.

CHAPTER 4/CONCLUSION

Congratulations! You've now concluded the fourth chapter in the BizBuySell Guide to Selling Your Small Business.

- Section 1 provided an overview of the process and timeline involved in selling your business.

- Section 2 covered the details of screening and communicating with buyer responses to your sale ads and listings.

- Section 3 included steps and advice for introducing and presenting your business and building buyer enthusiasm and trust.

- Section 4 dealt with the important process of receiving a buyer offer and accepting a buyer's letter of intent to purchase your business.

- Section 5 detailed the essentials of the due diligence process.

Now you're ready to prepare for the final stage of selling your business, including final negotiations, sale closing, and the transfer of your business, all of which is described in the upcoming Chapter 5. The end is in sight!

CHAPTER 5

CLOSING THE SALE AND TRANSFERRING THE BUSINESS

Overview

This chapter takes you through the home stretch of the business-sale process. So far, you've taken these steps:

- You've set your goals and objectives and are clear about what you want out of the sale of your business. (If not, see Chapter 1)

- You prepped your business so it was ready to attract buyers (Chapter 2 will help you through this phase).

- You placed ads and received inquiries from interested prospective buyers (for advice on this phase, see Chapter 3).

- You took all the steps involved to screen inquiries for suitability and capability to buy your business. You obtained non-disclosure agreements before revealing your business name. You presented your business to your prospective buyer. And you received a purchase proposal in the form of a letter of agreement, which was followed by the in-depth process called "due diligence." (For advice on all the steps involved in this phase, see Chapter 4).

- Now your buyer has passed the buyer's examination and it's time to complete the final steps before closing the deal, handing your business over, and embarking on your post-sale goals.

This chapter describes the important steps in front of you.

In six sections, Chapter 5 covers:

1. Closing the sale and transferring your business
2. Understanding the purchase and sale agreement
3. Understanding financing and tax implications
4. Negotiating final terms
5. Conducting a smooth closing
6. Transitioning your business

Count on this chapter to guide you to the finish line of a successful business sale!

Key terms in this chapter:

SBA Loan: A form of business financing that involves a loan from an American lending institution that is guaranteed in part (usually from 50 to 80 percent) by the U.S. Small Business Administration through its 7(a) program. Because the SBA stands behind the loan in the event of default, loan approval is somewhat easier. The process, however, often takes longer because the borrower has to be approved both by the SBA and the lending institution.

Promissory Note: Also called a loan note or a note payable. A document that names the person promising to fulfil a loan obligation (called the promisor, the obligor, or the maker, signifying the person making the promise), the person making the loan and accepting the promise (the promissee), the sum of money being loaned (the principal amount), the interest rate, and the repayment terms.

Secured Promissory Note: A promissory note that gives the person making the loan (the promisee) a legal right to valuable promisor-owned assets (collateral) that can be seized should the buyer not make payments as promised.

Subordinated Position: Secondary rights to collateral offered as security in a loan, with first or senior rights already pledged to another lender who has first call on the assets.

Personal Guarantee: A personal loan repayment promise. Important when a seller-financed loan is extended to a business entity, in which case the seller wants the owner of the business entity and the owner's spouse (if the person lives in a U.S. state designated as a community property state) to personally guarantee the loan so the seller can pursue the buyer's and the buyer's spouse's assets as recourse if necessary.

Third-Party Guarantee: A loan repayment promise provided by a third party; usually requested when a buyer has few personal assets and accepted only after approval of the guarantor's financial statement and credit report.

Restricted Stock Share Endorsements: A protection put in place, upon legal advice, by those selling stock to a private corporation that requires a seller-financed loan; by restrictively endorsing stock shares they do not become the buyer's outright property until all debt is repaid.

Installment Sale: A sale in which payments are received over a time period of more than one year, providing the buyer the option to make deferred payments and possibly providing tax advantages to the seller who can spread taxable income over multiple years.

CHAPTER 5/SECTION I

UNDERSTANDING THE PURCHASE AND SALE AGREEMENT

When the due diligence investigation that follows a buyer's purchase proposal comes to a successful conclusion, it's time to move into the final – and very important – negotiations that precede a sale closing.

By this stage in the sale process:

- A buyer has chosen to acquire your business.

- The buyer's in-depth investigation has confirmed the purchase decision, and your own due diligence has confirmed that the buyer has the financial and business capability to complete the purchase.

- Now it's time to reach consensus regarding price, payment structure, price allocation (and the resulting tax implications), and all the other details that comprise the final deal.

To get you ready, this section details what's in a "purchase and sale of business agreement" so you'll know what to expect, where to negotiate, and why it's so important to call on the expertise of your accountant, your attorney, and your broker.

Step-by-step actions

Step I. Understand what a purchase and sale agreement covers.

The following chart describes the contents of the closing agreement. Be aware that this list provides only a framework and general definition of an agreement's contents. Behind many of the items lie details that require advice from trained legal experts, which is why your broker and your attorney are key partners at this stage.

- **For the simplest sales** – those involving very few and uncomplicated assets and a selling price of tens of thousands rather than hundreds of thousands of dollars – fill-in-the-blanks forms can be downloaded from online sites. Just enter "purchase and sale of business agreement" in a search engine for a range of options. Before using agreement forms, however, call on the expertise of your attorney. Requirements vary from state-to-state and you need to be sure the agreement you sign complies with the letter of the law in your region.

- **For all other sales,** expect the sale agreement to span many pages and to be accompanied by exhibits and attachments that address all the necessary points to be covered. Your broker will guide the process if you're using one. Otherwise, either your attorney or the buyer's attorney will write the first draft and the other attorney will review and suggest amendments – unless you and the buyer agree to both work with and split the legal fees of a single attorney.

SALE AGREEMENT CONTENTS	
Names	Names of the seller, buyer, and business including the location of each.
Assets	List of all assets included in the sale including fixtures, furnishings, equipment, machinery, inventories, accounts receivable, business name, customer lists, goodwill, and other items; also includes assets to be excluded from the sale, such as cash and cash accounts, real estate, automobiles, etc.
Liabilities	List of liabilities being assumed by the buyer, often including accounts payable; also includes a statement that the buyer assumes no liabilities other than those listed.
Closing date	Statement of the date the sale will close.
Price	Statement of the purchase price and how the buyer and seller agree to allocate the price among IRS-determined asset classes.

Adjustments	Detail of how the price will be adjusted on closing day to reflect prorated business expenses and, if inventory and accounts receivable are being sold, to reflect closing-day valuations.
Seller agreements	Detail of non-competition or covenant not-to-compete agreement, management consulting agreement, or the employment agreement that the seller will sign as part of the closing deal.
Payment terms	Description of the amount of cash to be paid on closing day, the amount payable following terms detailed in a promissory note, and the amount to be paid in other, defined future payments.
Security agreements	If a portion of the purchase price will be paid through deferred payments, the agreement will include a description of buyer-owned assets listed as loan collateral; personal guarantee requirements if any, and business-operation requirements to protect against business and asset devaluation before price is paid in full.
Inventory	A list of all inventory included in the sale.
Accounts receivable	A description of accounts receivable included in (or excluded from) the sale, accompanied by a description of how payments for collections will be applied and how uncollected receivables will be handled.
Seller's representations and warranties	A statement verifying the seller's power and legal right to authorize the sale; that the seller has clear and marketable title to assets being transferred; that financial records presented fairly reflect the financial condition as of the date of the statements; that the seller knows of no obligations or liabilities beyond those disclosed as exhibits accompanying the purchase agreement.
Buyer's representations and warranties	A statement verifying the buyer's power and legal right to authorize the purchase; warranties that statements made by the buyer and buyer's guarantors contain no untrue statements or omissions.

Seller's covenants	A statement of provisions the seller will undertake to transfer the business including transferring employee benefit plans, paying employee wages through the closing date, changing the seller's business name to permit the buyer to legally assume and begin using the name, and other agreed-upon actions.
Employee termination clause	A statement confirming that on closing day seller will terminate all employees except those with transferable contracts, paying all wages, commissions, and benefits earned through the termination date, at which time the buyer will likely complete paperwork to hire terminated employees through the buyer's new business, which will have a new federal employee identification number (FEIN).
Post-closing rights and obligations	A statement of after-sale issues, likely including the buyer's right to offset the purchase price by liabilities or inventory valuation variances that become apparent after the settlement date; and the buyer's obligation to fulfill specified requirements such as carrying insurance, maintaining specified working capital levels, and allowing the seller to access financial records until the purchase price is paid in full.
Default provisions	A definition of litigation and dispute resolution provisions for dealing with defaults should either the buyer or the seller not fulfill the terms of the agreement.
Business transfer agreements	These agreements include the bill of sale; assignments of leases, contracts and intellectual property; stock transfer (for entity sales); statement of compliance with state bulk sales law requiring supplier notification (for asset sales)
Participation or absence of brokers	A statement of whether or not brokers or finders were involved in the transaction and, if so, how they'll be paid, which is usually stipulated in the broker agreement and usually paid by the seller on closing day.
Obligation for fees	A statement of how the buyer and seller will pay professional fees involved with the sale closing.

Step 2. **Prepare to negotiate the details.**

The preceding chart leaves little doubt that the purchase agreement is detailed and extensive. It's also the basis of negotiations between you and your buyer – not only about price, but also about exactly what's included in (and excluded from) the purchase and how the agreed-upon payment will be paid and allocated among IRS-defined asset categories.

The next two sections provide advice to consider prior to and during the negotiation process.

- Chapter 5/Section 2 gives you an overview of various payment structures and financing approaches – and the tax implications of each.

- Chapter 5/Section 3 provides tips for conducting the negotiations that precede the final goal of a smooth sale closing.

Resources:

Form, Link to Sample Purchase Agreement; http://www.bizbuysell.com/fsbo/resources/restricted/sample-purchase-agreement.pdf

Form, IRS Instructions for Form 8594/Asset Acquisition Statement; http://www.irs.gov/instructions/i8594/index.html

CHAPTER 5/SECTION 2

UNDERSTANDING FINANCING AND TAX IMPLICATIONS

Before you can understand the importance of negotiating the details of the purchase and sale agreement, which is the focus of the next section in this chapter, it pays to brush up on facts about how sales are financed and how proceeds are taxed. Why? Because every decision regarding the payment structure affects when and how money transfers from the buyer to the seller and how the payments are taxed.

No one is asking you to become a financing or tax pro. That's what your sale advisors do, and you'll want to call on their advice through every step from here through to the closing of your deal and the transition of your business to its new owner.

Content in this section aims to provide you with basic information to help you understand the advice you're receiving from those who are trained and up-to-date on the legal, financial, and tax implications of small business sales.

Step-by-step actions

Step 1. Understand the implications of each purchase-payment approach.

Each payment approach provides either you or the buyer – but rarely both of you – an advantage, which means every decision translates to a financial benefit to one or the other, and therefore a point of negotiation.

The following chart provides an overview of the approaches for funding and paying off small business purchases. Your broker or your accountant will be able to provide more in-depth information and descriptions for how the approaches affect your particular sale.

Payment Approach	Description	Cautions
Cash Payoff at Closing	Though rare, all-cash at closing eliminates concern about the buyer's ability to make after-closing payments.	An all-cash payoff has the potential to move you into a higher tax bracket, since you receive all proceeds as revenue during a single tax year. It also limits the buyer pool to those with cash resources or the ability to obtain cash through third-party loans. Research shows that cash-at-closing sales generally result in lower selling prices.
Third-Party Financing	Third-party loans allow the buyer to obtain the required down payment or to pay for the business at closing.	Bank loans are increasingly hard to come by and time-consuming to obtain. If during pre-screening a buyer indicates need for a third-party loan, request a prequalification letter from a lender prepared to provide the funding. Also, in advance of the sale, contact your bank or SBA office to learn whether and how the purchase of your business sale might qualify for an SBA loan.
Home Equity Loan	Homeowners can self-finance purchases by tapping the equity in their residences through a second mortgage.	If the buyer requires a home equity loan to provide the source of the closing-day down payment, and if you provide a seller-financed loan for all or some of the outstanding balance, don't accept the buyer's home as loan security since you'll have a *subordinated position* should you need to call on the asset.

| Seller-Financed Loan | By offering to accept deferred payments through a seller-financed loan, you attract more prospective buyers, ease and speed up the purchase transaction, convey faith in the future of your business, and, as a result, tend to obtain a higher purchase price. You also spread sale proceeds over multiple years, which may spare you from taxation at higher rates.

A seller-financed loan is detailed in a promissory note that explains the repayment promise and loan terms. | By signing a secured promissory note the buyer gives you legal right to valuable assets – collateral – you can seize as recourse if loan repayment terms aren't met. Beware of collateral in which you take a subordinated or secondary position. Also, beware of accepting business assets as collateral, as they can become devalued before you seize them. Should we mention that the business itself is often collateral for the seller loan, which means the seller gets the business back if the buyer defaults?

By requesting a personal guarantee as loan security (and buyer's spouse's personal guarantee as well, if they live in a community property state) you obtain a personal repayment promise that allows you to pursue personal assets as recourse if necessary. |

Earn out Payments	By agreeing to accept part of the purchase price based on how well the business does in the future you enhance business attractiveness by demonstrating faith in its future. You also reduce closing day cash requirements and provide yourself with a negotiating chip that often protects sale pricing. Further, you spread sale income over multiple years, which may provide a tax advantage.	The earn out must be defined in the purchase and sale agreement, including when payments are to be made, how they're to be calculated, and whether earn out payments are subject to minimum and maximum amounts. Most agreements stipulate that "calculations must be made by an independent certified public accountant mutually agreeable to the parties." Yet, this approach is risky, as your loan payments are subject to default, if the new owner fails at sustaining the business.
Stock Exchange	If your business sells to a corporation, the buyer may want to execute the purchase using stock rather than cash.	Be aware that there are typically process and time restrictions that limit when you can sell the stock you receive, and that unless the stock is widely and heavily traded a sale at a high price may be difficult.

Step 2. Understand the tax implications of how you receive and allocate purchase price payments.

Here's where your advice from your accountant can really pay off. Before agreeing to the payment approach and price allocation, be sure to get professional advice on the following topics:

- How you can qualify for tax deferrals by accepting part of the purchase price in installment payments over upcoming years and by allocating deferred payments to assets that will be taxed at capital gains rates.

- How you can allocate the purchase price among IRS-defined asset classes to avoid taxation at the highest rates. The IRS requires that you and the buyer both report the price allocation identically, using Form 8594. The allocation must follow IRS stipulations, and it also must win agreement from you and the buyer. Price allocation becomes a point of negotiation because tax advantages hang in the balance. Some allocations will benefit you. Some will benefit the buyer. None benefit you both at once. Again, don't proceed without professional advice from your accountant.

The following chart provides a quick overview of the seven IRS-defined asset classes, along with the rules and tax implications that apply to each.

ALLOCATING THE PURCHASE PRICE AMONG IRS-DEFINED ASSET CLASSES	
Class I assets: Cash and general deposit accounts	All cash that is transferring as part of the sale.
Class II assets: Actively traded personal property	The current-market value of all certificates of deposit, foreign currency, government securities, and publicly traded stock that will be transferring as part of the sale.
Class III assets: Accounts receivable and debt instruments	Accounts receivable, credit card receivables and loans due to your business if those assets are transferring as part of the sale.
Class IV assets: Inventory and stock in trade	The value of inventory and stock, which must be defensible based on cost or fair market value. The buyer may want to allocate as much as possible to this asset class because it qualifies as a deductible business expense.

Class V assets: Tangible/Physical assets	The value of furniture and fixtures, buildings, land, vehicles, and equipment that is transferring as part of the sale. The buyer will benefit from allocating as much as possible to assets in this class, which will qualify as business expenses or to which short-term depreciation rates apply. Conversely, you'll benefit from allocating as much as possible toward appreciated assets you've held long-term, which qualify for taxation as capital gains.
Class VI assets: Intangible assets not including goodwill	The value of all the non-physical assets of your business (not including goodwill), such as workforce, business books and records, systems and procedures, intellectual property, customer lists, and other assets that the IRS details in Form 8594 instructions (see link on this page). Frequently intangible assets are purchased in return for a non-compete agreement and/or a personal services contract, each of which offer different tax implications. Payment for a personal services contract allows the buyer to deduct the price as a business expense, while it will be taxed as ordinary income on your return for the year the payment is received. Payment for a non-compete agreement must be amortized or deducted over 15 years even if the agreement is for a much shorter time period, making it less attractive to buyers but more attractive to sellers.
Class VII assets: Goodwill and going-concern value	The value of goodwill is determined by math and negotiation. This asset class equals the purchase price minus the amount allocated to all other classes. You'll want to allocate as much as possible to goodwill because the proceeds will likely be taxed as capital gains.

The information in this section is necessarily detailed and extremely important since taxes, and therefore net dollars to you as the seller, hang in the balance.

One last time: This isn't the time for guesswork. Ask your attorney and/or accountant for advice before negotiating the final deal, which is the topic of the upcoming section in this chapter.

Resources:

Form, Instructions for Form 8594/Asset Acquisition Statement under Section 1060; http://www.irs.gov/instructions/i8594/

CHAPTER 5/SECTION 3

NEGOTIATING FINAL TERMS

Step-by-step actions

Here's what buyers know or think:

- You've priced your business on your own based upon emotional attachments.

- The down payment or amount of cash you receive on closing day is practically as important as the overall purchase price.

- In the end, the price will be determined by what the buyer is willing to pay and what the seller is willing to accept.

- Everything is negotiable.

With those thoughts in mind, realize that the buyer most likely approaches closing day with an intention to arrive at the best possible deal before signing the final purchase and sale agreement. And, likely, you intend to do the same. This section helps you through the back-and-forth, give-and-take that leads to the buyer's final offer and your final acceptance.

Step 1. Be ready for the negotiations in front of you.

Don't begin negotiations until:

- **You have a signed letter of intent** outlining the buyer's proposal and, if necessary, your counter-proposal.

- **Your sale advisors have provided you with legal and accounting advice** regarding the sale structure, price structure and price allocation that offers you the greatest financial benefit at the lowest tax liability.

- **You are clear about your own financial objectives** including the amount of money you want to receive at closing and whether or not you're willing to accept deferred payments by offering a seller-financed loan.

- **You know the issues that absolutely must be addressed** for the deal to go through. Some call these your deal-breakers. Others call them your knock-out factors, or your walk-away points. Perhaps you have a price figure you're not willing to go below. Or an amount you absolutely must receive at closing. You don't want to be unreasonable, but if you clarify limits before entering negotiations you'll know when, to say yes and when not say no.

Step 2. Be clear about what your negotiation needs to achieve.

Between now and closing day you and the buyer need to agree upon the issues in this chart, which you can refer to as a checklist:

✓	PRE-CLOSING NEGOTIATION CHECKLIST
	What's being purchased: The assets of your business, which will be transferred into a new business entity formed by the buyer (called an asset sale); or your business entity and all its assets and liabilities (called an entity sale).
	The purchase price, which will likely be 70-90% of the asking price, according recent data on BizBuySell.com.
	How the price will be paid, including how much will be paid at closing and how much, if any, will be paid through a seller-financed loan or deferred payments including earn out payments (see Chapter 5/Section 2).
	How the price will be allocated among the IRS-defined asset classes (see Chapter 5/Section 2).
	How to address issues discovered during due diligence, whether through price concessions or actions that rectify conditions of concern.

	How to handle the transition period, including how and when to contact customers and clients, whether employees will be rehired and how and when the sale announcement will be made, how suppliers, vendors and distributors will be notified, how work in progress will be completed, and how unknown liabilities that become apparent after the sale will be addressed.
	Your post-sale involvement with the business, covering such details as transition period involvement, timeframe and compensation, if any; post-sale involvement through a personal services contract; and your willingness to sign an agreement or covenant not-to-compete.
	How contingencies will be addressed/removed. These include such conditions as issues that arose during the due diligence investigation, acceptable transfer of leases and contracts, acceptable bank financing and other contingencies detailed in the letter of agreement to purchase.

Step 3. **Be ready to start and keep negotiations moving.**

Delays kill small business sales — especially during the negotiation process.

To keep negotiations moving, start by having all the information you need, including:

- The buyer's purchase proposal in the form of a signed letter of intent.

- Advice from your broker, if you're using one, and your attorney and accountant on each of the points in the preceding chart.

- Clarity about your personal objectives and limits.

Once you begin negotiating details, consider this advice:

- **Use your objectives as a steering device.** If you need to concede on one point, negotiate an offsetting advantage on another point. This advice applies particularly to price negotiations. If you need to settle for a lower price, your sale advisors can help you balance the concession by structuring the price for greater tax advantage or by altering the payment terms to reduce collection risk.

- **This isn't the time to increase your asking price.** You may begin to think your business is worth more than you asked, but don't try to increase its price during negotiations.

- **This isn't the time to get complacent about protecting your interests.** By this stage in the game you may almost feel in partnership with your buyer. Still, don't let your guard down when it comes to requesting personal guarantees and collateral agreements to back a seller-financed loan; or to request ongoing access to business financial records until the loan is repaid.

- **This definitely isn't the time for ultimatums or one-sided victories.** It's safe to assume that if you've gotten this far, you both want the deal to close. So aim for a win-win conclusion by offsetting each of your necessary demands with a compensating buyer advantage, and by working together to address the issues necessary to meet both your objectives.

- **Keep things moving quickly.** During negotiations you'll need to call a few timeouts in order to obtain input from your sale advisors regarding legalities and tax implications. When doing so, obtain the necessary information in the same day if possible. Delays either dampen interest or heighten concern – neither of which supports the kind of healthy negotiations that lead to a victorious closing day, which is the subject of the upcoming section in this chapter.

CHAPTER 5/SECTION 4

CONDUCTING A SMOOTH CLOSING

Once you and the buyer negotiate the fine points of the deal, explained in the preceding chapters, it's time to schedule the sale closing. This section details what you need to do in advance, during, and immediately following the big day.

Step-by-step actions

Step 1. Prepare for closing day.

Here's a chart outlining pre-closing day tasks. Work with your broker, if you're using one, and your attorney and accountant to confirm and take the steps necessary in your particular closing. Once each step is taken, review the closing-day materials with the buyer to ensure advance agreement for a smooth closing.

✓	PRE-CLOSING DAY CHECKLIST
	Schedule your closing when all parties are available and preferably during a morning hour so you can reach banks and government offices following the closing. Also, aim for the last day of the quarter, month or pay period to simplify proration of monthly expenses that transfer with the sale.
	Finalize the purchase price to reflect the outcome of price negotiations; prorated rent, utility and other fees; final inventory value; final accounts receivable and accounts payable value.
	Prepare corporate documents. If your business is structured as a corporation, work with your attorney to pass a corporate resolution authorizing the sale.

	Prepare government and tax forms, such as: Forms required by your Secretary of State or Corporations Commission; transfer documents for vehicles included in the sale; transfer documents for intellectual property; and prepare IRS Form 8594, which you and the buyer need to complete showing an identical allocation of the purchase price.
	Confirm insurance requirements detailed in the purchase and sale agreement.
	Prepare furniture and equipment sale list, accompanied by a list of which, if any, are under lease. Also prepare a list of assets excluded from the sale based on buyer-seller negotiations.
	Prepare to transfer contracts and agreements. Obtain approvals, assemble titles and leases, and take steps necessary to transfer all assets and obligations included in the sale.
	List and prepare to transfer work in process.
	Finalize list of accounts receivable and accounts payable, including aging reports.
	Prepare loan documents including a promissory note; security agreements including buyer's personal guarantee and personal guarantees from buyer's spouse and third-party guarantor, if any; and a UCC financing statement to be filed with your state.
	Prepare to transfer building lease. Assemble copies of lease and lease amendments; prepare lease assignment and assignment-acceptance documents.
	Prepare personal agreements including consulting or management agreement and covenant not to compete, if any.
	Prepare exceptions to warranties and representations, if any.
	Prepare succession agreements for employee benefit plans including profit sharing, flexible spending or other plans.
	Prepare the bill of sale.
	Prepare the closing or settlement sheet, which lists the purchase price and all costs and price adjustments to be paid by or credited to the seller and buyer. Your attorney will prepare this sheet unless your sale is closing through an escrow agent, in which case it will be prepared by the escrow office.
	Prepare the purchase and sale agreement.
	Other, based on input from your sale advisors.

Step 2. Schedule the closing.

If your sale will close in an escrow office:

- The closing will follow the instructions provided when the escrow account was established.

- The escrow officer will confirm that all obligations and contingencies listed in the letter of intent to purchase and in the escrow instructions have been addressed.

- You and the buyer will sign closing documents.

- The escrow agent will transfer funds and record the sale.

If your sale will close in an attorney's office:

- Your attorney, your buyer's attorney, or both, will prepare and review the purchase and sale agreement.

- Upon legal advice, you'll address any outstanding obligations or contingencies.

- You, your buyer, and the attorney who drew up the documents will meet to sign documents and transfer funds.

Step 3. Prepare and review the purchase and sale agreement.

Your broker, if you're using one, will likely provide a purchase and sale agreement form, or you can obtain one from a legal forms resource. Better yet, have your agreement drawn up by an attorney and – under any circumstances – have your attorney review the agreement before you sign it, since it contains descriptions of obligations that are regulated by rules that vary from state to state.

Chapter 5/Section 1 details the issues addressed in the purchase and sale agreement.

Step 4. Finalize the deal in a closing ceremony.

On closing day, here's what to expect:

- **Here's who will attend:** You and any other owners of your business; your spouse and any spouses of other owners of your business (necessary if you live in a community property state); your buyer or buyers and their spouses (necessary if they live in a community property state); third-party loan guarantors (if any) unless they previously signed personal guarantees or provided powers of attorney to those in attendance; your attorney and possibly your buyer's attorney; your escrow agent, if any; your broker, if you have one; and any others whose signatures will be required.

- **During closing, you'll likely take the following steps:**

- Agree to post-closing final adjustments to purchase price to account for prorated expenses and closing valuation of inventory and accounts receivable, usually finalized within 15 days of closing

- Review and sign the purchase and sale agreement.

- Review and sign loan documents.

- Review and sign lease-transfer documents, vehicle ownership-transfer documents, franchise documents, succession documents and other documents involved in transferring your business or its assets.

- Review and sign seller's consulting, employment, and/or non-competition agreements.

- Review and sign the bill of sale.

- Review and sign articles of amendment to change the name of your business, thereby freeing the name for use by the buyer. This step allows the buyer to amend the working name he or she has been using during the purchase process to the name being purchased as part of the sale.

- Review and sign forms to transfer patents, trademarks, copyrights and other intellectual property assets.

- Review and agree to the closing or settlement sheet listing all financial aspects of the sale including how expenses and credits are assigned to each party.

- Review and agree to the Asset Acquisition Statement, IRS Form 8594 (see Chapter 5/Section 2), which you and the buyer must attach, showing the identical allocation, to your federal income tax return.

- Receive the buyer's payment for the purchase price in full or for a sizable down payment, depending on the payment terms you negotiated.

And, with that, your deal is done! But your involvement isn't over. You still have to announce the sale and take care of long lists of details and legal actions necessary to formally transfer your business and ease its transition to its new owner. That's what the next two sections in this final chapter of the *BizBuySell Guide to Selling Your Small Business* are all about.

CHAPTER 5/SECTION 5

TRANSITIONING YOUR BUSINESS

The ink is now dry on the signature lines of the purchase and sale agreement. Money has passed from the buyer's hands into your bank accounts. Your business and its name are now owned by your buyer.

It's time for you to move into your new role – whether that means an all-new chapter in your life or an all-new relationship with your business and its new owner.

First, though, you have a long list of post-sale paperwork and actions to undertake in order to transition business operations to the buyer and close up what is now a shell of your business structure. Your attorney and your broker will guide you through this final post-closing activity. Here's what to expect.

Step-by-step actions

Step 1. Immediately after closing, provide the buyer with all information necessary to assume operation of your business.

What used to be your business now belongs to the buyer. That means you need to turn over all information that allows the buyer, now the owner, to assume its operations, including:

- Alarm codes.

- Computer, software and online access codes and passwords.

- Safe combinations.

- Customer, supplier, vendor, and distributor lists and supporting information.

- Keys to locks including building doors, vehicles, files and cabinets.

- Operating manuals for all equipment.

- Your personal contact information (if you aren't remaining during a transition period), including where to send all material required by the purchase and sale agreement.

Step 2. If your business was structured as a corporation or LLC, take legal steps to dissolve your business entity.

The vast majority of small business sales take the form of asset sales in which the buyer acquires all but specifically excluded assets of the business, including its name.

If your business was formed as a sole proprietorship, following the sale it will close automatically once you wind up business operations by following advice in the upcoming step.

But if your business was structured as a corporation or LLC, you have to dissolve your business entity:

- Meet with your board, partners, or members to pass a resolution to formally dissolve the business.

- Notify the IRS within 30 days of dissolution, using Form 966.

- File articles of dissolution with the state where your business was formed and any other state where it is registered.

Step 3. Complete forms and actions to cease operations of your business entity.

Rely on legal advice for the following steps:

- Notify contacts for all contracts that are being assigned to or assumed by the buyer.

- Notify creditors to explain how bills will be paid, either by you or by the buyer.

- Cancel business permits or licenses, assumed business names, and other registrations.

- Give cancellation notice on your lease if it isn't transferring to the buyer.

- Cancel insurance policies not being assumed by the buyer.

- Pay off bills and collect accounts receivable not being assumed by the buyer.

- Distribute assets remaining in your business after the sale closing, either to yourself if your business is structured as a sole proprietorship, or to shareholders, partners or members the business is a corporation or LLC.

- Close your employer ID number with the IRS.

- Close business bank accounts and credit cards.

- Close business line of credit, if any.

- Pay final wages to employees, and payroll taxes and fees due to tax authorities.

- File necessary tax forms, using the IRS "Closing a Business Checklist" featured as a link on this screen.

Resources:

IRS Closing a Business Checklist; http://www.irs.gov/businesses/small/article/0,,id=98703,00.html

IRS Form 996: Corporate Dissolution or Liquidation; http://www.irs.gov/pub/irs-pdf/f966.pdf (must be filed within 30 days of corporate dissolution)

CHAPTER 5/SECTION 6

ANNOUNCING THE SALE AND INCREASING THE ODDS OF FUTURE SUCCESS

Your deal is done. Congratulations!

There's no strategic reason for you to keep news of your sale quiet anymore, though buyers of restaurants or retail shops sometimes shield customers from the news until a transition period is complete and concern over a client exodus appears unnecessary.

In announcing the sale, consider this advice.

Step-by-step actions

Step 1. Tell your employees.	Either immediately before or after sale closing, tell key employees before making the announcement to all staff. If you can, avoid email in favor of a personal presentation made by both you and the buyer.
	Stress that the announcement is confidential for a limited time during which customers, suppliers and others must be notified.
	Briefly explain why you're selling. Just as the buyer wanted to know, so will your staff.
	Introduce the new owner, explaining your confidence in the buyer's expertise and plans before turning the floor over to the buyer to explain how employees will transfer to the buyer's organization; the buyer's plans for continuing business as usual (if so) and for embarking on growth plans (if any); and plans to meet individually or in groups with employees over the coming days and weeks.
	Describe the timeline, including when the sale will be made public (and therefore how long confidentiality is required) and when you, personally, will be departing.

Step 2. **Tell customers, suppliers, and business associates.**	First share the announcement personally with key clients, suppliers and business associates, including those whose support is most valuable to the business. Move quickly, because you won't want these important contacts to learn the news from others, media reports or competitor communications.
	Next make a general announcement, contacting individuals directly if the list is short or via an email or regular-mail announcement if the list is long. In your announcement, provide an upbeat, positive explanation that conveys enthusiasm and confidence. Explain that with great pleasure and after considerable planning you're pleased to announce that your business has a new owner. Introduce the owner through short description that conveys your confidence in the buyer's expertise and plans. Share a short statement about why you sold, what you're doing next, and how long you'll remain with business, if you will. Include a copy or link to a complete announcement, perhaps attaching the news release you'll distribute to media outlets.
Step 3. **Announce the sale to news outlets.**	If appropriate, prepare a news release or sale fact sheet whether you feel news outlets will carry the announcement or not. Doing so will put all facts into a single document you can distribute to local publications and broadcast stations, as well as to blogs and industry-specific news outlets.
	In the release or fact sheet, present who to contact for more information (and how), when the news can be released, the date of the announcement, a headline summarizing the announcement, and a clear presentation of facts. Consider also including a quote from you or the buyer and a photo of the buyer.

Step 4. Move aside.	Even if you remain with your business during a transition period or thereafter, the business now belongs to a new owner. Help staff, customers and business associates transfer their confidence to the buyer of your business, and move yourself out of the visible leadership role unless your agreed-upon ongoing role specifies otherwise.
Step 5. Move on.	You've done it. You sold your business! Now it's time to set a new goal. Chase a new dream. Buy a new business. The choice is yours. Congratulations!

CHAPTER 5/CONCLUSION

You've completed the final chapter in this *BizBuySell Guide to Selling Your Small Business*.

- Section 1 outlined the contents of the purchase and sale agreement that you and the buyer sign to complete the deal.

- Section 2 gave background information on how sales are paid for and financed, along with the many related tax implications.

- Section 3 focused on negotiations, including how to prepare for negotiating with your buyer, what points to cover, and what decisions must be agreed upon before closing day.

- Section 4 was all about the sale closing, including how it is scheduled, what's required, and what to expect from beginning to end.

- Section 5 lists what to do and legal steps to take as you transition your business to the new owner.

- Section 6 offers advice for announcing the sale and launching a successful future.

Selling your business is one of the biggest financial transactions many small business owners ever undertake. Best wishes for your future success.

Resources Page:

Recommended Reading & Resources:

Helpful Tools:

BizBuySell Broker Directory; (http://www.bizbuysell.com/business-brokers)

BizBuySell Valuation Report; (http://www.bizbuysell.com/business-valuation-report/)

National Trends in Small Sale Prices; (http://www.bizbuysell.com/news/media_insight.html)

IRS Instructions for Form 8594/Asset Acquisition Statement; (http://www.irs.gov/instructions/i8594/index.html)

IRS Form 996: Corporate Dissolution or Liquidation; (http://www.irs.gov/pub/irs-pdf/f966.pdf)

Sample Forms:

Business Sale Offer and Acceptance Agreement; (http://www.bizbuysell.com/fsbo/resources/restricted/business-sale-offer-and-acceptance-agreement.pdf)

Buyer Confidentiality Agreement; (http://www.bizbuysell.com/fsbo/resources/restricted/buyer-confidentiality-agreement.pdf)

Confidentiality Disclosure Registration Agreement; (http://www.bizbuysell.com/fsbo/resources/restricted/confidentiality-disclosure-registration-agreement.pdf)

Letter of Intent; (http://www.bizbuysell.com/fsbo/resources/restricted/sample-letter-of-intent.pdf)

Non-binding Letter of Intent; (http://www.bizbuysell.com/fsbo/resources/restricted/non-binding-letter-of-intent.pdf)

Purchase Agreement; (http://www.bizbuysell.com/fsbo/resources/
restricted/sample-purchase-agreement.pdf)

Recommended Articles:

Article, *Choosing a Business Appraiser*;
http://www.bizbuysell.com/seller_resources

Article, *Confidentiality Breach Can Ruin a Business Sale*
http://www.gaebler.com/Confidentiality-Breach-Can-Ruin-Business-Sale.
htm)

Article, *Documents and Information Required for Selling a Business*;
http://www.bizbuysell.com/seller_resources

Article, *Evaluation Rules of Thumb*;
http://www.bizbuysell.com/seller_resources

IRS Closing a Business Checklist;
http://www.irs.gov/businesses/small/article/0,,id=98703,00.html

Article, *Keeping it Confidential*;
http://www.bizbuysell.com/seller_resources

Article, *Seller Financing Basics*;
http://www.bizbuysell.com/seller_resources

Article, *Should You Sell It Yourself or Hire an Intermediary?*;
http://www.bizbuysell.com/seller_resources

Article, *What Impacts the Purchase Price of a Business For Sale*;
http://www.bizbuysell.com/seller_resources

Recommended Books:

Selling Your Business For Dummies written by Barbara Findlay Schenck (same author who helped write this Guide).

Built to Sell (http://www.builttosell.com) by John Warrillow; Built to Sell details how to build and sell a profitable, automated, efficient business.

EXIT! (http://www.exitjourney.com) Written by Julie Gordon White, a successful Business Broker in California; Julie highlights twelve steps to sell your business for the price you deserve.

Get Your Business Funded: Creative Methods for Getting the Money You Need (http://mrallbiz.com) by Steven D. Strauss; For those sellers interested in learning more about Seller Financing, be sure to read Chapter 20 (Pages 165-172).

Restaurant Dealmaker: An Insider's Trade Secrets for Buying a Restaurant, Bar or Club by Steve Zimmerman.

http://www.restaurantrealty.com/restaurantdealmaker.shtml

Made in the USA
Lexington, KY
26 May 2017